'Here something new and special has been written about univ
formation through higher learning often falls short of its prom
notes, but it is an immensely rich process and in many ways it forms the
societies. If *The Question of Conscience* is widely read we will have another reason to be
optimistic about the future of higher learning, additional to those rightly identified
by Watson in this thoughtful and accessible book.'

Professor Simon Marginson, joint editor-in-chief, *Higher Education*

'If one had to purchase a book that covers the world of higher education with all its
diversity of missions, structures, and dilemmas, then this is it. Elegantly written, it
draws on empirical research, history, philosophy, and literature to reaffirm higher
education's contribution to the cultivation of humanity.'

Rajani Naidoo, International Centre for Higher Education Management,
University of Bath

The Question of Conscience

IOEPress

The Bedford Way Papers Series

A full list of Bedford Way Papers, including earlier books in the series, can be requested by emailing ioepress@ioe.ac.uk

The Question of Conscience

Higher education and personal responsibility

David Watson

Institute of Education Press
Bedford Way Papers

First published in 2014 by the Institute of Education, University of London,
20 Bedford Way, London WC1H 0AL

www.ioe.ac.uk/ioepress

British Library Cataloguing in Publication Data:
A catalogue record for this publication is available from the British Library

ISBNs
978-1-78277-026-8 (paperback)
978-1-78277-051-0 (PDF eBook)
978-1-78277-052-7 (ePub eBook)
978-1-78277-053-4 (Kindle eBook)

Typeset by Quadrant Infotech (India) Pvt Ltd
Printed by CPI Group (UK) Ltd, Croydon CR0 4YY

Cover: Radcliffe Observatory, 1772–94. Kevin Nixon/University of Oxford

Contents

For Lila (born 13 April 2009)

Foreword

A famous science research professor in China was recently described as 'a frog in a well' after he had publicly dismissed a student as 'a silly liberal-arts girl'. He received about five thousand protests, condemning him because his narrow expertise had made him so 'ignorant of the wider world'. The trouble is that we have all been educated to be frogs in a well, specialists who, if we come out of the well, are confronted by mountains of knowledge, of many kinds, that we can never hope to master and also by oceans of injustice, misunderstanding, and exclusion to which we have no easy answer. That is the challenge that higher education faces. How can it possibly meet all the expectations that weigh on it, to foster not just learning, but also character and generosity? Sir David Watson's deeply thought-through book is an enormously stimulating and encouraging answer to this question. He uses his exceptionally wide knowledge and experience of many forms of post-secondary education, as well as of engagement with social problems, to review a huge range of ideas and practical experiments in this field, and to illuminate their potential.

Sir David demonstrated in Brighton how a university could raise professional training to a higher level and become a catalyst for local community innovation. His advocacy of lifelong learning is bearing fruit. In Oxford he is guiding the practical application of academic research to international problems of hunger and health. It is no longer enough for universities simply to prepare the young for existing jobs. Many professions are in crisis and demoralized. Many complain that bureaucracy is choking them. Many are organized on principles invented a long time ago that impose methods of work that no longer suit the aspirations of the new generations, who are more educated, more easily bored by routine, more adventurous in their interests, more cosmopolitan, less subservient and less willing to remain with the same employer for life. Not only is unemployment hitting the young very hard today, but the shortage is likely to get much worse as a billion more of them join the queue in the coming decades. Every time the world's population has exploded, new kinds of work have had to be invented, and it is urgent that universities include that in their agenda. Graduates need a more promising prospect than just competing against each other in an overcrowded market, begging for work from employers whose values they do not necessarily share. There are still a vast number of soul-destroying jobs for which no amount of work–life balance can compensate. It is a rare privilege to have work that expands one's horizons and gives one a sense of doing something really worthwhile, so that one would be willing to do it even if one was not paid.

Who can invent work that will satisfy the students whose curiosity and imagination and critical powers we have stimulated? It is they who will have to build their own world. Business is preoccupied with short-term profitability and government with winning the next election, but universities can think about the long term: they now have a new mission, helping students to shape the future of work.

That means reshaping how we use our time, and our greatly extended expectation of life. Over the past century, progress has meant roughly halving the number of hours spent at work in a lifetime and quadrupling the number of hours available for family, leisure, culture, and travel, with many more years being allocated to education. But we are also introducing more stress, or new kinds of stress, into work, and the kind of work we do has a more dominating influence on the quality of our existence and the opportunities open to us because our destiny is no longer so decisively determined by who our parents were. Work has to be refashioned to suit contemporary ideas of what a human being is capable of becoming, so that it furthers our deepest spiritual, moral, and cultural aspirations rather than obstructs them. Just to help the young to earn a living is not enough: too many talents are being sacrificed to meet purely industrial and commercial needs that ignore individual originality. Nor can students go to university just to 'discover themselves'. Sir David rightly adds, they need to discover others.

There was a time when universities could claim to be repositories of a consensus about how to live and what to admire, whether they were inspired by a religious legacy or were expressions of the enlightenment ideal of progress. But the ideologies of the past are losing their appeal. Many students do not know what they want to do with themselves; they may criticize the consumer society but have no clear alternative; and their professors are far less likely to be the revolutionaries with magic solutions that they might once have been. Not everybody can go into the City to make money, or get a job in the media or in an NGO. A career is no longer the enticing prospect it once was. As this book shows very powerfully, there is now unprecedented disagreement about what universities are for. That has advantages. It discourages mere imitation of traditional patterns and it justifies experimentation.

The age of utopias is over. So is the age of specialization that fears to look beyond its own frontiers. Universities are now social laboratories investigating what else they can offer students in addition to mastery of a single branch of learning. They can help them discover the realities of occupations other than those in which they are themselves involved, so that they can pioneer alternative futures for themselves based on knowledge of other people's problems and not just their own. Students can be encouraged to expand the content of their conversations and the diversity of their interlocutors systematically, to search for unused potential in others, and to forge links between superficially disparate individuals so that they do together what they cannot do alone. Beyond their present focus on finance and management, business schools have an important part to play in facilitating interaction between isolated faculties. They can use their contacts with the worlds of both work and scholarship to assume a more conscious role as interpreters and intermediaries between them. They can develop broader syntheses of human experience in ways that point to untried possibilities. Achieving expertise is less likely to be frustrating when it is coupled with a search for wisdom. And now for the first time in history there is the prospect of work being reconceived to reflect women's needs as well as men's traditions.

Of course, it is not easy to avoid being a frog in a well. We have habits that prefer to continue on familiar paths in institutions that are often tempted to make self-preservation their supreme goal. But there are now new kinds of opportunities for interaction between teachers, students, and the outside world. That is how the New Learning of the Renaissance penetrated into England in the sixteenth century: a few dons with a few students in a small college began studying what no one else was studying, drawing inspiration from neglected sources. That too was how original research into contemporary issues was introduced into universities in the twentieth century, in collaboration with practitioners from outside of academia and from foreign countries. With about three million students following courses outside their own country, and far more using the internet, universities have become major players in the expansion of imaginations. This book shows that small groups are already experimenting around the world, trying out new methods, new programmes, and new collaborations. The future for universities may seem dark because of financial constraints and insatiable demands, but it is bright because never have so many people turned to them hungry and thirsty for a fuller life.

Theodore Zeldin, CBE, Commandeur Legion d'Honneur
Emeritus Fellow, St Antony's College, and Associate Fellow, Green Templeton College, Oxford

Acknowledgements

Early versions of the arguments here were given as the fifth annual Drapers' Lecture at Queen Mary University of London in October 2010; to seminars at the University of Oxford Department of Education during the academic years 2010/11, 2011/2012, and 2012/13; to a group convened by the Vice Chancellor of the University of Melbourne in August 2011; to the Open University 'inclusive higher education' conference in April 2012, as parts of successive Presidential Addresses to the Annual Conference of the Society for Research in Higher Education (SRHE) (2010, 2011, and 2012); as contributions to the Higher Education Policy Institute (HEPI) series of House of Commons seminars in 2011 and 2012; and to the twentieth anniversary conference of the Staff and Educational Development Association (SEDA) in May 2013. 'The long march of the professional formation university' (the basis of Chapter 4) was originally shared with the Centenary Conference of the School of Education at the University of Brighton in September 2010, and 'the ethical idea of the university' (the basis of Chapter 3) with Newman University College in May 2008. I am grateful to participants on all of these occasions for their advice. Chapter 6 draws significantly on the work of the Inquiry into the Future for Lifelong Learning (IFLL), which I was privileged to chair in 2007–9, and whose report was published as *Learning Through Life* (Schuller and Watson, 2009). The 'pedagogies' section of Chapter 1 draws on work conducted with the team looking at transitions to postgraduate study funded by the Higher Education Academy (HEA) and led by David Scott at the Institute of Education (see Scott *et al.*, 2013). Other parts were first published as 'The University and its Student Communities: knowledge as "transformation"?' in Paul Temple (ed.) *Universities and the Knowledge Economy* (Routledge 2012).

In addition to the further development of ideas I have first proposed in other books and articles (all referenced below) I would also like to thank the editors of *Perspectives: policy and practice in higher education, Educational Review, Higher Education Review, The London Review of Education, Lifelong Learning in Europe, Times Higher Education*, and *The World Yearbook of Education* for giving me space to preview some more recent thinking and permission to re-work some of the material here. It has been a pleasure to work again with Jim Collins and the Institute of Education Press, and I am particularly grateful for the incisive comments on my initial proposal by the Press's three referees. My title is a deliberate echo of *The Question of Morale* (Watson 2009). In that book I tried to set out how the modern university works, including – at its best – as a complex pattern of tacit and explicit mutual commitments by its members at various times. The focus of *The Question of Conscience* is what all of this noisy, argumentative – but at heart fundamentally principled activity – is for; especially with respect to the university's graduates as they make their way into the world.

David Watson

As usual, friends and colleagues have argued with me about smaller and larger parts of what is here. I am deeply honoured that Theodore Zeldin has agreed to contribute a foreword. His *An Intimate History of Humanity* (Zeldin, 1994) provides a model for the kind of history I aspire to write; at one stage I considered attempting to make this book 'an intimate history of the university', but knew that I would fall short of the model. I do, however, endorse the central conclusion of Theodore's masterwork: that in spite of (and partly because of) the dilemmas we face, we in higher education have more options in front of us than we currently believe to be the case.

The democratic ethos of Green Templeton College (GTC) has created the opportunity to test most of my ideas with students and fellows, especially over lunch and dinner, including parts of the Preface at a dinner seminar in November 2012. Vice-Principal Ingrid Lunt and Fellow Emeritus John Lennox have been particularly valuable intellectual companions. The early parts of Chapter 6 were tested with a seminar of GTC alumni in September 2011 addressing the question of 'is HE worth it?' The image on the front cover is of 'Tower of the Winds': copied from Athens by James Wyatt for the Radcliffe Observatory in 1772, it now stands at the heart of the College, and is a wonderful physical reminder of the cultural 'layering' I write about in Chapter 1. Much of my understanding of the wider educational and social context also comes from the learning I have drawn from working with my fellow-trustees, staff (especially Josh Hillman, Anne Hagell, and Sharon Witherspoon), and the researchers we have funded from the Nuffield Foundation.

I have, as usual, drawn upon the resources of the incomparable Library of the Institute of Education, University of London, as well as continuing conversations with my former colleagues at the Institute's pioneering Centre for Higher Education Studies (CHES), notably Ron Barnett and Paul Temple. For Ron the university will always be in the mind; in his latest book, *Imagining the University*, he writes about the value of 'hopeful fictions … never to be fully achieved', but 'nevertheless energizing the university in the direction of desirable journeys' (Barnett, 2013: 160). For Paul it will always be on the ground: in a recent article he reminds us of 'the need to integrate these and other conceptual aspects of higher education with understandings of operational matters' (Temple, 2012: 318).

While absolving them of any blame for what is wrong in what follows, I am grateful to all of these friends and fellow travellers, and especially to Betty Pinto Skolnick. My dedication is to our granddaughter, Lila Watson Parekh, already tuning up to be part of the matriculating class of 2027.

Oxford and Lewes
1 July 2013

List of acronyms

AAAS	American Academy of Arts and Sciences
AAUP	American Association of University Professors
AKU	Aga Khan University
APR	Age-related Participation Rate
AUA	Association of University Administrators
AUW	Asian University for Women
BBC	British Broadcasting Corporation
CATS	Credit Accumulation and Transfer
CDBU	Council for the Defence of British Universities
CHES	Centre for Higher Education Studies
CIHE	Council for Industry and Higher Education
CMI	Chartered Management Institute
CNAA	Council for National Academic Awards
DES	Department of Education and Science (UK)
DfE	Department for Education (UK)
ECTS	European Credit Transfer System
EI	Emotional Intelligence
EQ	Emotional Intelligence Quotient
ESRC	Economic and Social Research Council
ERA	Education Reform Act
EU	European Union

FE	Further Education
GMTV	Good Morning Television
GSP	Graduate Standards Programme
HE	Higher Education
HEA	Higher Education Academy
HEAR	Higher Education Achievement Record
HECSU	Higher Education Careers Support Unit
HEFCE	Higher Education Funding Council for England
HEI	Higher Education Institution
HEPI	Higher Education Policy Institute
HEQC	Higher Education Quality Council
HESA	Higher Education Statistics Agency
ICT	Information and Communication Technologies
IER	Institute for Employment Research
IFLL	Inquiry into the Future for Lifelong Learning
IOE	Institute of Education (London)
IPPR	Institute for Public Policy Research
ISMC	Institute for the Study of Muslim Civilisations
LSE	London School of Economics
MBA	Master of Business Administration
MIT	Massachusetts Institute of Technology
MOOC	Massive Open Online Courses
MPP	Masters in Public Policy

NCIHE	National Committee of Inquiry into Higher Education
NHS	National Health Service
NSCH	National Student Clearing House
NSS	National Student Survey
NUS	National University of Singapore
NUS	National Union of Students
ODL	Open and distance learning
OECD	Organisation for Economic Cooperation and Development
OU	Open University
PPE	Philosophy, Politics, and Economics
PSHE	Public Sector Higher Education
PSB	Professional and Statutory Bodies
PSI	Policy Studies Institute
QAA	Quality Assurance Agency for Higher Education
QMUL	Queen Mary University of London
QR	Quality-related research (funding)
RAE	Research Assessment Exercise
REF	Research Excellence Framework
SCAA	School Curriculum and Assessment Authority
SCOTCAT	Scottish Credit Accumulation and Transfer
SCQF	Scottish Credit and Qualifications Framework
SEDA	Staff and Educational Development Association

SEECC	South East England Credit Forum
SOMUL	Social and Organisational Mediation of University Learning
SQA	Scottish Qualifications Agency
STEM	Science, Technology, Engineering, and Mathematics
SRHE	Society for Research into Higher Education
TAFE	Technical and Further Education (Australia)
TAOTPR	The Art of Taking Personal Responsibility
TA	Teaching Agency
UBC	University of British Columbia
UCL	University College London
UKBA	United Kingdom Border Agency
UKCF	United Kingdom Credit Forum
UUK	Universities UK
WBL	Wider Benefits of Learning

List of figures

About the author

David Watson has been Principal of Green Templeton College and Professor of Higher Education at the University of Oxford since October 2010. He was Professor of Higher Education Management at the Institute of Education, University of London, from 2005 to 2010, and Vice-Chancellor of the University of Brighton between 1990 and 2005. His most recent books are *Managing Civic and Community Engagement* (2007), *The Dearing Report: Ten years on* (2007), *The Question of Morale: Managing happiness and unhappiness in university life* (2009), and *The Engaged University* (2011).

'My trade' and why it matters

Insider or 'participant' observation poses some familiar problems for the exercise of social scientific judgement. A personal framework is set here for what follows in the bulk of the book, based as it is as on self-reflection and an intended level of disciplined self-study.

My trade

This is a book about what higher education institutions (chiefly universities) say they have been doing for and to their most important members (their award-seeking students) and why it matters. On a personal note, contributing to this process and these ambitions has been my trade for nearly forty years. However, the book aims to be much more than a personal odyssey (I have set that out elsewhere, in Watson 2011). I am intrigued by how varied these claims have been over the long history of the higher enterprise, but also by how strong and determined they invariably are. Essentially the argument here is that such claims represent a moving combination of recurrent themes, nearly all present at the creation of the modern university, and liable individually to wax or wane according to mainly (but not exclusively) external influences.

The centre of gravity is my own experience of the UK system, but the analysis is also informed by conversation and experience around the global enterprise of higher education as well as reliance on those who have written compellingly about it. Methodologically it may seem to draw upon an odd and potentially unstable mixture of evidence: my personal experience (including of management as well as more dispassionate investigation); what the best of the research literature tells us; the perspectives of think tanks and lobbying groups (including the notorious university 'gangs' identified in Chapter 7); fiction and personal memoirs; as well as journalism (popular and professional) from around the world. However, I have tried to identify in each case the strength of the warrant for the views expressed, and I trust that surrounding some of the trickier issues with this range of voices is more illuminating than not.

In his version of *My Trade: A short history of British journalism*, the political correspondent Andrew Marr states: 'Now I turn around, and find I've been doing this strange apology for a proper job for more than twenty years.' He goes on to say that '[s]omehow, somewhere along the road, journalists stopped being shabby heroes, confronting arrogant power, and became sleazy, pig-snouted villains. ... Has something turned rotten in the state of journalism or is that only what all ageing hacks believe' (Marr, 2004: xxiii).

There are strong echoes here of the volumes on those shelves in the higher education section of university libraries stuffed full with the memoirs of former presidents, vice-chancellors, and principals. They too, invariably say 'I slipped into this', before going on modestly to describe their triumphs (with just enough Maoist self-criticism to keep the reader on board, they think). Personality shines through here. Compare, for example, the self-critical reflection of Donald Kennedy of Stanford (*Academic Duty*) with the bombast of Stephen Trachtenberg of George Washington (*Big Man On Campus*) (Kennedy, 1997; Trachtenberg, 2009). A comfortable majority are also declensionists, in the sense of being theorists of decline. Like the 'ageing hacks' nothing is likely to match the contributions of 'their' era. Historical analysis will, however, as usual cast doubt on the validity of more than one golden age.

My first confession has to be that as a witness to this claim and charge I am seriously institutionalized. I went to University (Cambridge) in the 'revolutionary' year of 1968 after an inspiring stint teaching in Julius Nyerere's then hugely promising Tanzania. I have never left the peculiar world of higher education since then. I got my first serious senior management jobs in higher education in the late 1970s and early 1980s, including at Oxford Polytechnic – now the very successful Oxford Brookes University. I have returned after 20 years to Oxford to lead the 'other' University's newest College, Green Templeton: the result of a unique piece of Oxford's 800-year history, it is the only formal merger between two previously independent Colleges. Green Templeton's merging of the traditions of health and clinical medicine on the one hand, and modern management and organizational behaviour on the other, with a selection of critical social science disciplines in the middle, makes it intellectually and professionally one of the most exciting places to be in one of the most exciting universities in the world.

In between these book-ends I spent fifteen enormously satisfying years as Vice-Chancellor of the University of Brighton, helping that place to grow into what is probably Britain's most successful large 'professional formation' university, and another five at the Institute of Education of the University of London, where (following George Bernard Shaw) I briefly gave up 'doing' higher education management and tried to 'teach' it.

This means that I have lived through – and had to adapt to the eleven new 'frameworks' imposed on the UK higher education system by successive governments since the *Robbins Report* of 1961. The Coalition Government's White Paper of June 2011 is the latest. We are, as Rachel Bowden and I once wrote at the height of New Labour's legislative activism on HE, the 'fruit-flies' of the international higher education laboratory (Watson and Bowden, 2005). For us in the UK it means that the system has been radically reconfigured for every third or fourth new cohort that has entered it. The reason for this, and the real failure in the process, is that of corporate or policy memory. Come back Cassandra, all is forgiven.

It also means (yet another 'contradiction') that I remain an optimist. I don't think that you can be an effective educator for a long time without keeping at least a small, non-cynical, amelioristic flame alive. Every one of those new cohorts counts, and every one of them deserves your best.

Who 'runs' our universities?

So who is responsible, who picks up this profound obligation or, more prosaically 'who runs our universities?' This was a challenge laid down to me by the editors of *Perspectives*, the journal of the UK Association of University Administrators (AUA) in 2012, for their fiftieth anniversary. How does 'my trade' work?

The editors may have come to me because I have a bit of form with topics like this. In 2008 I challenged the Quality Assurance Agency for Higher Education (QAA) with the question 'who owns the university?' I concluded that nobody owns the university forever, and almost everybody (across the range of various categories of members, through investors, to supporters) could claim to own parts of it from time to time (Watson 2008a). In 2009 I went further (at book length) in trying to answer the question 'who decides what the university is for, and how?' My conclusion was that the situation is very complicated, and, of course, that more research is needed. The list of candidate stakeholders is long, even if the 'risk' attached to their various stakes is variable from the intense (students) through the ambiguous (employers in general) to the non-existent (parts of the media). University governance – in the sense of ultimate responsibility for the institution – is required to balance all of these voices (Watson 2009: 84–96).

Inside the academy there is a cultural perspective that it should run itself, in the sense that 'business as usual' should be done with no one's hands obviously on the levers. This theory reaches its high point in the 'self-government' of Oxford and Cambridge Colleges (and in a slightly different way in the governance of these two universities).

This is what can spook a number of interests outside the academy. They suspect we are out of control; or that the wrong people are in control. In fact, Oxford and Cambridge are in this respect, as in many others, *sui generis*. Among their principal theorists are David Palfreyman and Ted Tapper, whose latest work, *Oxford, the Collegiate University*, is unashamedly a work of advocacy, for the revival and maintenance of a world the authors think is almost lost. Their concept of the Collegiate University is rooted in the experience of the richer 'mixed' (i.e. predominantly undergraduate) Colleges identified by the Franks Commission of the 1960s and North Committee of 1997. These 12 'richer' Colleges (there are 30 'mixed' Colleges overall) are seen as carrying the 'College' torch in determining the character of the University. Its essential elements include the provision of undergraduate teaching (notably the tutorial), the maintenance of what A.H. Halsey termed 'commensality' (covering the broader aspects of the environment, including buildings as well as food and drink), and strict self-governance. To survive, 'collegiate universities' are seen as having to meet five 'preconditions': independent self-governance; control of membership; provision of 'a social and cultural setting' for members; 'ideally' financial independence (although dependence should never lead to 'compromising policy decisions'); and fulfilment of key functions (so, for example, they remain 'actively engaged in teaching, learning and research') (Tapper and Palfreyman, 2011: 167).

The authors have the good sense to recognize this model for what it is: an invention of the Victorian era. Cardinal John Henry Newman is its principal theorist: 'A university embodies the principle of progress, and a College that of stability; the one is the sail, and the other the ballast; each is insufficient for the pursuit, extension and inculcation of knowledge; each is useful to the other ... It would seem as if a University, seated and living in Colleges, would be a perfect institution, as possessing excellences of different kinds' (Ibid. 27). However, it is important not to romanticize what the model consisted of. As discussed in the next chapter, in the context of contending pedagogies, the modern Oxford tutorial, for example, began as a form of remedial education for not very bright middle class young men.

This essentially late nineteenth-century model of the ancient University is now under strain, from several directions: from the development of the University (especially through scientific research as a countervailing power); from the vicissitudes of public policy (especially related to funding); from public expectations more generally in an era of mass higher education (especially in relation to access and social justice); and from what is seen as intrusion into the private business of both College and University governance.

In most other settings (i.e. away from Oxbridge) the academic estate is seen more regularly as contributing to 'shared governance', in the sense that the peculiar circumstances of higher education institutions require a structured cooperation between academic and corporate interests: the former representing the mainstream, everyday business (of admitting members, making awards, and authorizing research); and the latter satisfying funders about the application of their contributions, ensuring the viability, and setting the 'character and mission' of the institution (Shattock, 2006: 58–80).

In reality most Universities are run through a delicate – and relatively exceptional – pattern of interleaving and overlapping fields of 'governance, leadership and management'. Governance is the exercise of stewardship of the institution as a whole, within a framework set by the institution's foundation and ongoing legal and/ or constitutional status. This will also include ultimate responsibility for strategic direction. Governance is thus also about setting the conditions for and holding to account the leaders of the organization. Leadership is about setting the conditions for and then coordinating and motivating the performance of the institution. The third element of the trinity is Management. This has a much more operational feel: it is about doing the right things and doing them well. Crudely, if governance is about stewardship, and leadership is about stretch, then management is about institutional strength (Watson, 2009: 118–22).

Individuals may, of course play various roles across these broad categories, sometimes simultaneously. The resulting lines of authority will then look complex and essentially non-hierarchical. In our *Managing Institutional Self-Study*, Elizabeth Maddison and I suggested that the resulting organizational chart would look more like a doughnut than the traditional, hierarchical organogram, as follows (based upon the University of Brighton):

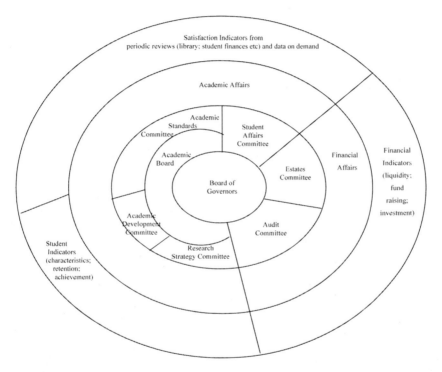

Figure 0.1: University of Brighton management and governance

Source: Watson and Maddison (2005): 34

Then there is the phenomenon that in the 'flat', professionally argumentative communities that constitute our universities, almost everyone manages other people and in turn are managed themselves, sometimes switching roles more than once during the course of the day: as teachers, committee chairs or members, researchers, administrators, ambassadors, sales-persons, stewards, and so on (Watson, 2009: 129–34).

The resulting tensions are played out in a kind of semi-public dance around and between at least three totem poles.

The first is about *autonomy*. UK universities are proud of their relatively high (by international standards) institutional autonomy. They are formally independent corporations, or persons in law. They hold this autonomy at the institutional or corporate level (their constituent parts – like faculties and departments – have none of the legislated privileges that they enjoy in some parts of continental Europe). British HEIs can use their assets for their chosen purposes, with the exception of some – now almost all paid-off – elements of certain 'Treasury-funded assets'. They employ all of their own staff. However, they also enter (formally at will, practically through various elements of *force majeure*) public contracts that bring compliance conditions, and they have recently (for about the past twenty-five years) become addicted to earmarked funding, or competitive 'initiatives' (the first casualty of the current recession).

The second is about *accountability*. Except in certain highly ideological quarters there is a general understanding that the academic community has to take in its own washing, collectively, on matters of standards in the making of academic awards. This leads on to a series of controversies about regulation and quality assurance.

And the third pole concerns *academic freedom*. Universities – to deserve the name – have to be free to follow difficult ideas wherever they may be. But they also have to be prepared to test their conclusions and to explain. As I have argued, in American constitutional terms, it is a first amendment and not a fifth amendment freedom (Watson, 2009: 123; see also Chapter 7).

In these circumstances a series of reality checks are in order.

First, there is the issue of what universities were set up to do. What, more precisely, were their *founders' intentions*? And how important do they remain? Historical analysis underlines the fact that nearly all university-like institutions grew out of and were supported, at least initially, by host communities of various kinds.

There is an important corollary: under what circumstances can the management and leaders of the day decide to do something entirely different? In most cases the founding fathers (not that all were male) did not set out to be as high as possible up the 'world-class' league tables; nor to drive out all of the opposition. Universities were established to be significant players in civil society, simply by 'being there'.

In *Managing Civic and Community Engagement* I tried to develop and refine a model for understanding university–community relationships. This has essentially three axes: first-order engagement, which arises from the university simply 'being there'; second-order engagement, which is structured around contracts and formal agreements of various kinds; and third-order engagement, which is the relationship between the university and its members (Watson, 2007).

The second reality check – very much in tune with contemporary discourse – concerns the issue of *who is paying* for it all. Who puts the university in funds to do what?

In many cases, this leads to 'second order' engagement, constructed around contracts, with their own conditions of procurement, of process, and of delivery.

There is a wide variety of relationships here: from the very substantial contracts with the Higher Education Funding Councils, the Teaching Agency (TA), and the National Health Service (NHS); through various 'sealed' arrangements with individual companies, employers, and professional bodies; to simple one-off arrangements, like standard-testing.

Again there is a corollary, in terms of the conditions under which the university holds funds, for example in the form of endowment. The Charity Commission has a supervisory role here. Oxford Colleges, for example, spend about 95 per cent collectively of the products of their asset portfolios on supporting annual expenditure (University of Oxford, 2011). That is one reason that they can claim to cost so much.

A mixture of 'first' and 'second' order engagement will give the university its activity, or business 'mix'.

In terms of *teaching* the mix will incorporate what students want to study, what the university wants to offer them, and what any other sponsors and (genuine – that is risk-taking) stakeholders want to support. The UK system provides ample evidence of how (despite political voices to the contrary) a market does exist. Indeed student choices – of subjects, of institutions, and of mode of study – could be said very substantially to have moulded the system as we have it today. That is how the system has adjusted to meet the needs of the creative and service economies, and that is why so many supply-side STEM (Science, Technology, Engineering, and Mathematics) initiatives have failed. That is why there is a slow but inexorable move towards studying closer to the family home. And that is why institutions (like the Open University), which hold out the prospect of earning while learning, are increasingly popular, even while they are arguably undermined by policy and funding priorities (Swain, 2012).

In terms of *research* it will depend on a mix of what choices the university can make for itself and (as in the case of teaching) how much they are prepared to chase the market. The Research Assessment Exercise (RAE) and its successor the Research Excellence Framework (REF) loom very large here. However, such is the concentration of funding that this has led to (and which is now objectively regarded as dysfunctional) that chasing improved scores and anticipating improved funding in a zero-sum environment has proved severely irrational. For all institutions other than the 'golden triangle' of Oxford, Cambridge, and some London-based institutions, the real game is away from the fruitless pursuit of increased Funding Council 'Quality-related research' (QR) (Watson and Maddison, 2005: 108–13).

And then there is the currently fashionable question of *service*, or of civic and community engagement. No HEI can now operate without some form of 'engagement' strategy, structuring its dealings with its communities at different levels (from the local to the global) and with Civil Society (Watson, 2007).

Thirdly, who ensures and stands behind the *quality* of the product? Again a number of elements interleave here.

There is the question of student (or consumer) satisfaction. Students – despite a lot of hype to the contrary – generally know that they are not simply customers. In our system, they cannot simply purchase a degree. They are, however, increasingly conscious of the 'hygiene' factors in choosing courses and institutions, and of their rights if institutions do not live up to their own standards of professional delivery and treatment. There is the question of academic and professional standards, not least the drive to have teaching in higher education professionally accredited.

And then there is the interplay between the reputation of the awarding institution and the quality of what it offers. Another aspect of student consumer awareness (and rationality) is that they will – if they are able to – often choose institutional reputation (where a place is in the pecking order of public understanding, media approbation, and perceived access to postgraduate networks) over the quality of what they might receive while studying. Meanwhile, to the frustration of some groups (such as the Sutton Trust in their 'wasted talent' mode), well-qualified students from non-standard backgrounds will often make the opposite choice: to study where they will be more comfortable, and quite possibly more personally supported as learners (Sutton Trust, 2008).

Fourth, and finally, what about the world outside? Universities are quick (and correct) to identify that they create public goods and serve the public interest. How is this interest crystallized at any particular time? How can it be reinforced or subverted by politics or fashion (including public confidence)? Are there circumstances in which simple institutional interests are trumped by the wider public or sectoral interests that universities characteristically claim to promote and defend? Henry Mintzberg concludes his latest account of the dilemmas of modern management with the simple, arresting question, '[h]ow about what is right for the organization being wrong for the world around it?' (Mintzberg, 2009: 224).

All of this creates a rich mix of issues for those who directly 'run' universities to deal with – that is their governors (or trustees), managers (at all levels) and leaders (again all across the community).

How flexible should a university be? How should it set a balance between what it sees as 'future-proofing' and historical stewardship? When and how should anyone decide that the game is up? Does a real university ever die, as opposed to adapt, or be absorbed? The second coming of Antioch College – one of Burton Clark's key cases in his classic work *The Distinctive College* – re-opening after closure appeared final, is a remarkable example of the principle of everlasting institutional life (Clark, 1970; Cowen, 2011).

Running through this preliminary analysis there have basically been two threads: one is about *resources* – who provides them, and with what intentions; the other is institutional *identity* – structured around ongoing, shared commitments, which can't be compromised. The first is about money; the second is about morality.

In Woodward and Bernstein's *All the President's Men*, Deep Throat's key piece of advice was 'follow the money', although, as Bob Woodward admits, he never actually used that phrase: 'I cannot find it in any of my notes. But that was certainly the idea' (Woodward, 2005: 70–1). In higher education this idea will get you some distance, but not all of the way. A better piece of advice in our world is to 'follow the award'. Universities give awards, like degrees, which cannot simply be purchased. They also validate the outcomes of research. In both cases they share between them commitments to standards and to academic honesty.

'Following the award' can expose some of the weaknesses of 'franchising', where institutions license others to award their degrees for money (and have even been known to allow secondary and tertiary layers of the same sort of relationship). The meltdown in 2011 of the University of Wales – the former mother-ship of a large federal system that had converted into an enterprise for which franchising was basically the sole business – is now a classic cautionary tale in UK HE (Matthews, 2012).

Following the award would have defused much of the brouhaha about A.C. Grayling's New College of the Humanities, which was launched with great fanfare and celebrity-soaked press releases, also in mid-2011. As the University of London pointed out in a quieter intervention, all that is happening formally is a group of academics (and their financial backers) deciding to prepare students (who will have to register individually) for the 'external' (now termed 'international') awards, for which the University will take responsibility for the syllabus and the assessment (University of London, 2011). If you are interested in who is 'running' this 'university', following the money (the mooted £18,000 fee) is the wrong trail. In its first year the NCH was planning to recruit 375 students; it opened in September 2012 with 60 (Hermann, 2013). Meanwhile, following the award also identifies the University of Cincinnati as having provided the lifeline for Antioch (Cowen, 2011).

The bottom line is that Universities are quintessentially membership organizations. Participation is voluntary – by students, staff and other 'partners'. These are the 'risk-sharers' who constitute genuine stakeholders. With the exception of the relatively new (in the UK) breed of 'for-profit' universities (designed, in the words of Harold Hotson, primarily to 'get the funding moving from federal [government] coffers to the student's debt ledger, through the university, and into the pockets of shareholders and chief executives'), the analogy with share-holding organizations just does not hold up (Hotson, 2011). However, they also have to live in a number of intersecting and overlapping worlds, which provide locations, contracts, and trade, and a wider community of knowledge exchange and use. Each of these worlds can impose their own (sometimes conflicting demands); their representatives can also occasionally over-step the mark. It is the duty of university governance, leadership and management to analyse, adjudicate, and steer through such choppy waters.

David Watson

Living with ambiguity

In other words, they have to live with ambiguity. On ambiguity, just over twenty years ago I took the classic literary formulation, William Empson's *Seven Types of Ambiguity* (1930) and ran through the list as it applies to our trade. The seven types are: meaning several things simultaneously; resolving two or more things into one; two ideas ... given in one word simultaneously; two or more meanings not agreeing among themselves; incomplete performance by the author; saying nothing; and having two opposite meanings. I was able to apply them fairly neatly to our sacred cows: quality, efficiency, teaching, choice, diversity, modularity, and the university (Watson, 1994: 81–2).

I want to tighten the ratchet further. We are susceptible not just to the ironic playfulness of ambiguity, but to the deeper consequences of error. And I want to pray in aid another classic text.

The Oxford philosopher Gilbert Ryle coined the term 'category mistake' in his *The Concept of Mind* (1949). He talks about a 'foreigner visiting Oxford or Cambridge for the first time'. He is:

> shown a number of colleges, libraries, playing fields, museums, scientific departments and administrative offices. He then asks 'But where is the University? [Incidentally, I have been asked exactly the same question on the streets of Oxford.] I have seen where the members of the Colleges live, where the Registrar works, where the scientists experiment and the rest. But I have not yet seen the University in which reside and work the members of your University'. It then has to be explained to him that the University is not another collateral institution, some visible counterpart to the colleges, laboratories and offices which he has seen. The University is just the way in which what he has already seen is organized. When they are seen and when their coordination is understood, the University has been seen.
>
> (Ryle, 1949: 17–18)

This passage is interesting on a number of levels, especially historical (the priority of the Colleges, the salience of the Registrar, the absence of explicit reference to students, the apparent lack of lecture halls, the scientists 'experimenting', and so on), but it is Ryle's first and strongest example of the 'category mistake'. The visitor mistakes the buildings for the concept: the infrastructure for the institution (Ibid.).

A classic dictionary defines the category mistake as follows: 'a sentence that says one thing in one category what can only intelligibly be said of something of another, as when speaking of the mind located in space' (one of Ryle's targets was Cartesian dualism of the mind and the body). Another gives the example 'what does blue smell like?'

I discern at least eight such category mistakes in today's discourse about higher education, its problems, and its prospects.

'University' performance

The first is about to what extent the individual university is the most sensible unit of analysis. Here we talk about the 'university' when what is actually in question is the subject, professional area, or the system in which the institution sits. Courses, subjects, and evolving inter- and multidisciplinary academic and professional fields, should count more than whole institutions (indeed a rather brittle, un-self-aware species of institutional pride can be a real problem). Examples are health and medicine, art and design, engineering and technology, which often share developmental problems across the sector more than they do with other disciplines in the same institution. The UK National Student Survey (NSS) has shown, for example, that differences in response between subjects – across all institutions – are much more marked (and statistically reliable) than differences between institutional aggregates (Ramsden *et al.*, 2010: para. 16.3).

Access

The second is about the admissions dilemma: is it about the pursuit of 'excellence', or more about 'social mobility', or even 'social justice'? Here we talk about 'widening participation' as if it is the same as so-called 'fair access', and *vice versa*. The two are logically separable phenomena. The first – getting more students qualified and to the starting-gate – is a big problem. The second – where they choose to apply, and are admitted – is a comparatively tiny problem. Merging the two can also lead to empirically weak and socially patronizing conclusions. As noted above, there is the related category mistake of the Sutton Trust in stating that well-qualified students choosing courses (and institutions) outside the golden circle of the 'Sutton 13' top universities (all from the Russell and 94 groups) are 'wasted talent' (Sutton Trust, 2008).

The higher education 'sector'

The third is about the scope of the 'sector' from the points of view of policy, of practice, and, critically, of self-image. This concerns talking about 'higher' when we should be talking about 'tertiary' education. In gross terms – and notwithstanding the wobbles we have seen recently in terms of so-called 'dual sector' provision (when what is called in the UK 'further' education, or in Australia Technical and Further Education [TAFE] takes place in the same institution as HE) – it is 'tertiary' (including higher education) rather than exclusively 'higher' education that matters to society at large. The emerging question internationally is how both higher and further education sit within frameworks of lifelong learning (Schuller and Watson, 2009). As an extreme example of new formations, the University of Peshawar in northern Pakistan sustains all levels of learning from nursery school to PhD (see the website in the list at the end of this book).

Research 'selectivity'

Next there is the myth of research concentration. This is not just about the stark conclusion that in the UK we have concentrated public funding of research to the point where it has become dysfunctional, but also involves talking about institutional research intensity when we should be talking about inter-institutional collaboration. As university leaders, policy-makers, and funders focus on league tables and so-called competitive advantage they are actually being undermined by the scientific community's ever-increasing tendency to cross boundaries. This is how the Royal Society summarizes the position:

> The scientific world is becoming increasingly interconnected, with international collaboration on the rise. Today over 35 per cent of articles published in international journals are internationally collaborative, up from 25 per cent 15 years ago.
>
> The primary driver of most collaboration is the scientists themselves. In developing their research and finding answers, scientists are seeking to work with the best people, institutions and equipment which complement their research, wherever they may be.
>
> The connections of people, through formal and informal channels, diaspora communities, virtual global networks and professional communities of shared interests are important drivers of international collaboration. These networks span the globe. Motivated by the bottom-up exchange of scientific insight, knowledge and skills, they are changing the focus of science from the national to the global level. Yet little is understood about the dynamics of networking and the mobility of scientists, how these affect global science and how best to harness these networks to catalyse international collaboration.
>
> (RS, 2001: 6)

Locally (in the UK) this should cause us to think long and hard about the upcoming Research Excellence Framework (REF). Two outcomes are certain in 2014. Hyper-concentration of funding in the hands of a few 'QR (quality-related)-winners' will continue: four HEIs will continue to scoop about 30 per cent of the spoils, and up to about 75 per cent. As a result we shall have to learn to live with a two-tier system. This division will not, incidentally, simply recreate the binary line: 'old universities' without medical schools will mostly be outside the charmed circle; 'new universities' will be well-placed to prosper in the second tier. The main effect of the REF will be to freeze funding in a state set somewhere between 2001 and 2007. Moreover, this appears to be the basic policy intention: much of the Higher Education Funding

Council for England (HEFCE) consultation about setting up the scheme was about 'stability' and avoiding 'perturbation'.

Two tiers will represent a policy trap for various reasons. Entry to the top tier will become virtually impossible. New combinations of subjects (and institutional partnerships) – the very stuff of 'foresight' at its best – will wither in this part of the sector. Above all, a radically divided system represents a counsel of despair: the best of what we have now is the best we can ever hope for.

Life among the QR winners will not, however, be a bed of roses. The real value of 'dual support' has been in steady decline since 1992, and genuine FEC (full economic costing) remains out of reach (Adams and Smith, 2007). Missions here will become narrower as internal concentration of resource mirrors external funding. They will also be increasingly dominated by medicine and science; not least because funding required to 'match' investments in science and technology will progressively bleed the arts and humanities.

The favoured institutions will find themselves more and more operating against the grain of a 'mode 2' world of knowledge creation and exchange. There will be disincentives to participate in academic partnerships that dilute the citation denominator (exacerbated, for example, by the treatment of group authorship as a single unit for the purpose of excluding self-citation). It is also likely that the QR-winners' relative decline in the ability to 'gear' or 'leverage' public money into private support will continue.

As for the rest of the institutions, life outside an inflexible and backwards-looking QR-winners' circle will have its compensations, as well as some ongoing challenges. The most important task will be to 'right-size' an approach to their own morsels of QR, that recognizes their relative contribution to a wider pool of research funding. Meanwhile a concerted effort must be made to demonstrate that institutional reputations (including for research) can be made away from the RAE/REF, which will cease to be 'the only game in town'. Such reputations will depend upon catching a number of waves: the increasing importance of the creative and service economies; a renewed interest in 'liberal' values in undergraduate education that fuses the research and teaching agenda; and a similar demand for 'translational' research (Gawande, 2007).

Together these developments will offer an alternative, forward-looking definition of 'research intensity'. Above all, they will mean adapting to a world of wider and deeper collaboration, in which at many of its scholarly frontiers the isolated institution is no longer the power it once was.

World-classness

Fifthly, this links directly with the madness of supposedly 'world class' provision, especially as identified by international whole-institution league tables. At present both politicians and institutional leaders (the latter should know better) are obsessed with a poorly designed concept of comparative 'world classness' when they ought to be talking about geographically specific 'engagement'. What governments say they want from higher education systems represents almost the opposite of what the international league tables they also exhort us to climb actually measure (see Salmi and Altbach, 2011).

I offer below two starkly different lists: of what governments at a variety of different levels say they want higher education to do and what the 'world-class' tables rely upon. Despite Herculean efforts, everything reduces to peer-reviewed research, and even that is problematic because of the inexorable rise of collaborative outcomes at the very highest levels of achievement. The game is given away by the *Times Higher Education* World University Rankings, which are 'designed to look at globally competitive research-led institutions'. When it comes to doing the sums, 'research' is in fact just about the only thing they measure: it represents nearly three-quarters (73.5 per cent) of the data they use, even though these are massaged into superficially more balanced parts of the description (*THE*, 2012: 4, 34–5).

There is today virtually no significant 'strategy' for any area of public policy (economic development, health, education, criminal justice, social cohesion, and so on) that does not include an important role for higher education. The sort of things these strategies search for are: high quality teaching and training, contributions to social mobility, services to business and the community, attention to rural as well as urban interests, collaboration across the range of the public services, and the public interest in general. None of these elements counts in the international league tables.

What does count in these rankings, based as they are in crude metrics and partial retrospective samples of esteem (the 'beauty contest' element), is peer-reviewed research, a certain amount of media interest, elite graduate destinations (especially political and business), the infrastructure (ivy-clad quadrangles help) and international recruitment to the more expensive 'executive'-style course. High volume recruitment to undergraduate courses – which can often serve to maintain specialist provision where domestic demand is precarious – has come to be seen not as a strength, but as a source of vulnerability.

Against this background, the system itself is reasserting its global and international activities, reach, and value systems, just at the same time as it is most rigorously exhorted to be local, regional, and national. Look for example, not just at the growth of collaborative research, but also at 'international' student cultures – including the 'virtual' – incidentally (and as discussed in Chapter 3) a descriptor for a type of university initially coined by Cardinal Newman.

The public–private divide
There is no clear blue water now (if there ever was) between the 'public' and the 'private' sectors: what often makes the difference is how the private sector can be used for public purposes. Meanwhile we have the ironic phenomenon that as

universities are urged to be more 'business-like' (admittedly on a rather outmoded version of what complex 'business' actually consists of), many successful businesses are becoming more 'university-like'. The whole domain of open-source software illustrates this while other specific examples of companies include Whole Foods, W.L. Gore, Google, and Linux (Hamel, 2007: 72, 95, 107, 111, 207–9)

Informed choice

Penultimately, we have to ask the hard question about who is really running the show. What students want and need can confound the most sophisticated policy frameworks, where spokespersons react to what they regard as irrational choices by prescribing more and decreasingly plausible 'information'. Look at the ways in which student demand led the systems of the 'developed' world towards meeting the needs of the cultural, creative, and service economies. Students' ICT requirements (where they are nearly always ahead of their teachers) compound this. As set out in Chapter 6, the UK system provides ample evidence of how (despite political voices to the contrary) a market does exist.

The public discourse is heavily dominated at present by a perception (whether welcomed or deprecated) of student instrumentalism. What counts is 'employability' (even more than 'employment') and whether or not students are prepared for it. Meanwhile students themselves confound expectation further: not just in choice of subject of study (as above), but by delaying their entry into the job market (when they can), by being much less concerned about debt than their parents (Surowiecki, 2011), by returning to volunteering (even while they simultaneously have to work much more frequently for money than their predecessors) and by reviving student-led political activism (all around the world).

Reputation and quality

Choice of institution is also a contested element, and leads to a final category mistake: the confusion of reputation and quality. In the United States, Andrew Delbanco concludes that 'the 'quality gap' between private and public universities is much smaller than the gap in reputation' (Delbanco 2007). Evidence is growing in developed systems that students are choosing 'reputation' over 'quality' in selecting universities, and that as long as employers screen for the same thing they are acting rationally in doing so.

Lawrence Blum (Professor of Philosophy at the University of Massachusetts) responded to Delbanco in terms that are worth quoting in detail:

> Institutions such as my own are outposts of serious and bright students of modest or low-income background taught by dedicated faculty who are often respected researchers as well. These institutions are home to a democratic institutional culture simply not possible at elite institutions

... It is time that the national agonizing about the income bias of elite institutions shifts its focus to these institutions.

(Blum, 2007)

These data and these conclusions are mirrored in the UK. The Higher Education Policy Institute's (HEPI) surveys of student classroom experience in 2006, 2007, 2009, 2012 and 2013 have observed 'the new universities if anything making more provision and in smaller classes than the old, and less likely to use graduate students as teachers' (HEPI, 2009: para. 10). While critics have raced to comment that the older universities are more likely to have graduate students available, the impact is confirmed by other reports. The ESRC's Teaching and Learning Research Programme's (TLRP) project SOMUL (the Social and Organisational Mediation of University Learning) concluded that 'you won't necessarily learn more if you go to a posh place' (SOMUL, 2005), while similar results have been reported more recently by Paul Ashwin (Ashwin *et al.*, 2011).

The combined effect of these category mistakes is to suggest that higher education research needs to put its own house in order. Not all of these eight failures of analysis (and of imagination) originate from outside the academy. In addition to telling truth to power (or at least the policy-makers temporarily in charge) we also need to focus on telling the truth to ourselves.

I don't pretend that these elements of necessary refocusing add up to any coherent theory – several are palpably self-contradictory – although I shall not give up looking for it. Examining the 'question of conscience' may provide part of the answer.

I would like to conclude these preliminary reflections on 'my trade' with a final subversive thought. The overheated battle between those inside and those outside UK universities about who is really in charge conceals a fundamental, objective truth. In comparative terms, and much as it may make us feel better to argue the opposite, especially in difficult times, nationally we are a 'lucky' system. Despite the pressures of a hyperactive political context, we have maintained a 'buffer' between ourselves and the government of the day. The provision of the 1988 Education Reform Act that the Secretary of State cannot make a grant in respect of an individual institution remains in force (ERA, 134:7). We have broadly been well funded at times, and less well funded at others (HEPI, 2006a). Public funding has not kept pace with expansion but it has increased in absolute terms decade after decade since the 1960s. Our levels of student satisfaction are relatively high compared to those in similar national sectors, although they may be slipping – for predictable reasons. The bar remains high on degree-awarding powers and university title, while – although they creak from time to time, the processes of mutual assurance of quality and standards remain intact. We have had very few Millennium Dome or Terminal Five moments, when compared to, say, the National Health Service; although Cardiff, Thames Valley, and London Metropolitan universities, and most recently the London School of Economics (LSE) may be exceptions proving more than one rule.

However, we are now entering another one of those periods (the late 1970s and early 1980s were the last) when we need to become a smarter system. We are facing another storm: of national policy confusion (exacerbated by devolution), of funding uncertainty, and of diminished public confidence. Survival and prosperity will once again only securely be achieved – as they have been in the past – by taking responsibility for 'running' our own affairs.

Outline: What does higher education seek to do?

This book explores the issues through at least five lenses:

- *the 'evolutionary' stages of modern university history;*
- *the sense participants and observers try to make of them in terms of institutional narratives;*
- *the types of 'capital' generated by their activities;*
- *the chosen pedagogical approaches; and*
- *a declared set of 'purposes', or intended personal transformations.*

The resulting combinations are sorted, or clustered, around five major 'questions' about the role of universities for their students, and in society at large. Conclusions are then drawn about the role of higher education in developing (or not) varieties of personal responsibility.

Historical strata (Chapter 1)

- Late medieval specialist communities
- Regional and national institutions serving post-industrial society
- Public 'systems' of HE
- Curriculum and institutional innovation
- The 'dual sector'
- 'For-profit'

Narratives (Chapter 1)

- Liberal
- Professional formation
- Research engine
- Business services
- National pride
- Civic and community engagement

Capitals (Chapter 1)

- Human
- Social
- Creative
- Identity
- Mental/well-being
- Spiritual

Pedagogies (Chapter 1)

- Dogmatic instruction
- Self-discovery
- Expert credentialism
- Service learning
- The practicum
- Research apprenticeship
- Lifelong learning

Purposes and transformations (Chapter 1)

- Religious confirmation/conversion
- Personal development
- Social (and political) engagement
- Technical competence
- Professional acculturation
- Networks
- Maturation
- Protected time
- Love of a subject
- Mental gymnastics

Questions

- The question of conscience (Chapter 2)
- The question of character (Chapter 3)
- The questions of calling, competence, and craft (Chapter 4)
- The question of citizenship (Chapter 5)
- The questions of conversation and of capability (Chapter 6)

A Hippocratic oath for higher education (Chapter 7)

- Strive to tell the truth
- Take care in establishing the truth
- Be fair
- Always be ready to explain
- Do no harm
- Keep your promises
- Respect your colleagues, your students and especially your opponents
- Sustain the community
- Guard your treasure
- Never be satisfied

Associated dilemmas (Chapter 7)

- Autonomy
- Advocacy
- Attitude
- Accountability
- Anticipation
- Advertising
- The arms race
- Ambience (and atmosphere)
- Access
- Asymptosis (always approaching)

Chapter 1

What does higher education do? A historical and philosophical overview

To attempt to capture a holistic view of the modern university is a foolhardy goal. Nevertheless the effort is made here to combine an account of where and how these peculiar institutions were founded, by whom and with what intentions, as well as the narrative senses the participants have tried to make of their enterprise (the history). These are then traced against various theoretical models (the forms of capital aimed for), practical and professional choices (the pedagogies), and claims for the outcomes. Finally, the outcomes are clustered into some pervasive or perennial questions (the philosophy).

University history as geology

The approach of this book is emphatically historical, and based upon a theory that the history of higher education is essentially geological. Strata are laid down at different times, in differing ways, and for different purposes, but once there are irremovable. In some parts of the university world they are nearer the surface than in others. 'Pipes' connect some locations directly with earlier layers. Here is how Roy Mottahedeh, a historian of Iran who now teaches at Harvard, describes one such set of pipes:

> I realised (and subsequent study confirmed) that my friend and a handful of similarly educated people were the last scholastics alive on earth, people who had experienced the education to which Princeton's patrons and planners felt they should pay tribute through their strangely assorted but congenial architectural reminiscence of the medieval and Tudor buildings of Oxford and Cambridge. Here was a living version of the kind of education (with its tradition of disputation and commentaries and super-commentaries on long-established 'set texts') that had produced in the West men such as saintly and brilliant theologian Thomas Aquinas and the intolerant and bloodthirsty grand inquisitor Torquemada, and in the East thinkers such as Averroes among the Muslims and Maimonides among the Jews

> (Mottahedeh, quoted in Muborakshoeva, 2013: 29).

Robert Alter uses the same metaphor in his 'story of the powerful afterlife of the Bible in the prose style of American fiction', *Pen of Iron*. It is a 'prime example of how any verbal culture remains dialogically engaged with its own earlier strata'. I would want to say the same thing about higher educational values as he does about verbal culture:

> In the evolution of verbal culture in particular, very little is altogether discarded. Once a text, together with the language in which it is cast, has been authoritative, that authority continues to make its force felt in the work of later writers, even those who no longer assent to the original grounds for the authority.

> (Alter, 2010: 4)

Other geological metaphors also work. For example, tectonic plates are formed that move slowly but sometimes cause major disruption. Strange deposits can result as the strata act upon each other.

Here are the main layers, as I see them (based on Watson *et al.*, 2011: Part I).

Phase 1: specialist communities

The early foundations were specialist communities, such as the late medieval colleges for poor scholars in England – Oxford (1167) and Cambridge (1209) – and for urban professionals, such as Bologna (1088), Paris (1170), and Salamanca (1218) in continental Europe. Stephen Lay points out that what distinguished all of these foundations from their ancient predecessors was the presumption of independence from state (or in some cases – like Paris – church) authority, creating conditions of what has subsequently become termed autonomy (Lay, 2004: 109). They provided a template for 'university' institutions for a long period during which activities that we would now regard as belonging to higher education – for example in early modern science – happened in other places (for example, through aristocratic patronage or private societies).

Phase 2: national and regional institutions serving post-industrial society

After this fallow period, the next significant wave of foundations took place in the nineteenth century. These grew similarly out of perceived social and economic needs, but in the radically different context of industrializing societies. Examples are the University of Berlin in 1810, the national universities founded by the European states, the late nineteenth-century 'civic' universities in the UK and the Land Grant universities of the American West and Mid West, established in the middle of the Civil War by the Morrill Act of 1862. The latter were progressively leavened by specific, primarily research-based institutions, on the German Humboldtian model, such as Johns Hopkins. In this process post-Enlightenment science, perceived economic need, and national (and regional) ambition fused together.

Nor was the effect confined to new institutions. Following the layering principle, older institutions, founded for different purposes, proved highly adaptable, including the leading American seminaries. Yale created its Sheffield Scientific School in 1860, having appointed its first engineering professor in 1852 and set up the inaugural Scientific School in 1854. Cambridge followed suit in 1875, and Oxford in 1908 (see websites).

Phase 3: public 'systems of HE'

In the next wave of development, the twentieth century saw the development across Europe and North America of university or college *systems*, sometimes regionally planned as with the English polytechnics and American state systems (of which the archetypes are Wisconsin and the Californian Master Plan). These were specifically tied to expectations about relevant education and training, with a new element of ensuring both access by groups previously under-represented, and their progression through the system.

In many countries, the result was to create what came to be known as binary systems of higher education: a group of traditional university institutions contrasted with a more local, apparently more locally accountable, and apparently more responsive pattern of provision. The 'binary question' is a hugely important one. In his 2008 lecture for the Higher Education Policy Institute in London, Yves Mény, President of the European University Institute, saw this division as largely constructed around the separate realms of research and teaching. It reached its highest form (and one of the rare instances in which teaching is seen as more significant than research in reputational terms) in France:

> In fact, in most continental countries this strict division of labour was put in place rather late and mostly after the Second World War. Indeed in France for instance, where the Napoleonic model was imposed in a radical way, the fundamental division was not so much between teaching and research but between the university system on the one hand and the professional schools in charge of educating and training the future civil servants of the State.
>
> (Mény, 2008)

Around the turn of the twenty-first century, this juxtaposition posed real dilemmas for policy-makers dealing with the advent of mass higher education. Those with binary systems felt that they had run their course; those without them felt that the only way to re-inject mission diversity was to try to create a polytechnic-style counterpoint to unresponsive autonomous universities; others who had tried the change decided they needed to change back (some of the recent institutional developments in Australia feel like this; South Africa may be doing the same thing). In the UK, the Labour Party's most sympathetic think tank, the Institute of Public Policy Research (IPPR) is the latest voice to suggest that 'large further education colleges providing higher education should be given the ability to award degrees and such colleges should be granted the renewed use of the title 'polytechnic' (IPPR, 2013: 9, 45–6).

Phase 4: curriculum and institutional innovation

To return to the *schema*, these were followed by late twentieth-century experiments in curriculum, pedagogy, and a further drive towards accessibility. Examples here are the pioneering of open access, or admission of adults without formal qualification by the UK's Open University and New York's City College system, and their imitators around the world. At the same time, developing nations began to establish the mega-universities, as defined by John Daniel, making use of open and distance learning technologies (ODL) to speed up participation, and to cut costs (Daniel, 1996). Open and distance learning is a key example of innovations surviving and being adapted across 'layers'.

Even the experiments in ODL built upon traditional foundations. In the United States there was the phenomenon of 'degrees by correspondence', begun by the University of Chicago in the last decade of the nineteenth century and picked up by California, Wisconsin, and Columbia in the early part of the twentieth (Noble, 2002). Between the 1920s and 1940s there was a vogue for courses offered by radio, led by New York University but also drawing in some of the more prestigious players like Harvard (Matt and Fernandez, 2013). In 2008 the University of London's external degree scheme celebrated 150 years of what has historically been called 'extension' or extra mural' business by supporting 43,000 students in 183 countries (Kenyon Jones, 2008: 35–50). What began as basically the use of new technologies (like correspondence and broadcast) to attract new types of students (particularly 'heroic', later in life, second-chancers) shifted to become a mainstream mode of delivery for established and conventional universities. Thus the British Open University has moved its basic platform from the British Broadcasting Corporation (BBC) to the internet-based iTunes (Watson *et al.*, 2011: 171–2), the Massachusetts Institute of Technology (MIT) has evolved its simple publication of course material online (beginning in 2002) into a sophisticated programme of custom-designed and assessment-friendly materials (see the MITOPENCOURSEWARE website), and institutions across the reputational range are lining up to join the MOOC (Massive Open Online Courses) movement.

Writing in the summer of 2013 MOOCs are on everybody's lips. The Coursera network (see website) now claims over a million registrations (although the organizers acknowledge that many of these will simply be browsing), followed by its rival Udacity (coiner of the term MOOC) at nearly three-quarters of a million (J. Young 2012a). Each of these brands has its founding gurus, like Sebastian Thrun (late of Stanford) at Udacity and his former students Andrew Ng and Daphne Koller at Coursera. They all play homage to Salman Khan, of the Khan Academy, which now has over ten million students studying mathematics around the world (Cadwalladr, 2012), although there were other pioneers like the 'connectivist' movement started by George Siemens and Howard Rheingold (of the University of Manitoba) in 2008 (see website), and udemy, founded by Eren Bali in 2010 (see website). The UK has moved to join in, led naturally by the Open University. It is taking the lead in a new enterprise – Futurelearn Ltd – in partnership with 11 other British universities (Open University, 2012). Another entrepreneurial intervention is a website offering to certificate the outcomes. 'Degreed is a free service that scores and validates your lifelong education from both accredited (i.e. Harvard) and non-accredited (i.e. iTunesU, Lynda.com, Khan Academy, etc.) sources' (see website). In California MOOCs are being mooted as a solution to the financial meltdown of the system of guaranteed progression to state institutions (Gardner and Young, 2013; Bidwell, 2013).

Nowadays a full fat MOOC implies, in addition to open access and modest or no fees, a robust platform (often based on shared or commercial software), an institutional sponsor, the option of assessment (and equally of ducking in and out at will), and at least theoretical accreditation of learner outcomes.

What disturbs many administrators and some (although fewer) teachers about MOOCs is the sense that they are not in control. This is simultaneously part of the attraction to students and some other interested parties. In this way MOOCs play their part in a long tradition of students (and a younger generation of academics) leading in the field by seizing technological aids for their studies while their institutions lag behind. Other examples would be learning through games and simulation, the creative use of proprietary software, the use for academic purposes of social networking, the transition from wired to wireless, and the shift from computers to telephony. Collectively, and long before teachers worked out what was happening, students were involved in all sorts of distance learning, often at very short distances indeed. One of today's most familiar sights in a university is two students sitting side by side, talking, and looking not at each other but down at the smartphones they hold in their hands. As usual (and they are not often asked) it is the librarians who will tell you what is really going on.

MOOCs are currently being taken up (or not) across a spectrum of activities and interests.

Enrolled *students* are of a wide variety of types. There are those who want to try courses out, or who 'alight' on material that may be relevant to their more regular academic work. Many of these are in effect sophisticated, selective and fundamentally partial consumers. They may be just down the corridor from the source (actually, or metaphorically, if they are registered in an institution like the provider). Then there are those for whom a free (or very cheap) MOOC is a lifeline; they will be much more likely to want to aggregate their achievements towards an award (from somewhere – remember 'follow the award'). They may be anywhere in the world. Yet others are in the tradition of lifelong learning autodidacts. They can be serial users; recent research has found evidence of MOOC accumulators in the high 20s (of number of courses taken) (J. Young, 2013b).

Then there are the *teachers* and course designers. The heroic individual trailblazers may now be being slipstreamed by a classically higher volume of 'early adopters'. Here control issues loom large: is a MOOC just a 'publication' or 'academic development' option undertaken by the faculty member or is it a serious potential risk to the reputation (and the brand-related earnings) of her employer? Surrounding them will be a combination of principled critics and 'deniers' (Schmidt, 2013). The arguments against MOOCs from within the academy will range from a genuine concern at the loss of intimacy on the student–teacher relationship; through the traditional 'not invented here' objection to the outsourcing of, for example, basic or introductory material (there was a similar outcry in the 1970s when the UK Council for National Academic Awards [CNAA] suggested widespread adoption by other institutions of Open University units); to a trade union-style concern about loss of market share, or poaching. All of these elements came together in a letter of protest signed by 58 Harvard professors against the arrival of edX in May 2013 (see below, and Kolowich, 2013).

Meanwhile one of the most interesting side effects of MOOCs is on pedagogical research (Agarwal, 2013). Practical issues include the following: new ways of 'scaling-up' up how to present material; techniques for avoiding cheating in assessment (e.g. by registering key-stroke-based learner identity); automated assessment (including the populist and long-standing moral panic of having 'computers mark essays'); ways of running highly distributed, sometimes carefully and strategically designed, social-networking enabled, learning groups; and (perhaps most productively) also testing the power of moderated peer assessment (another version of the wisdom of crowds).

Students and teachers work in and for and occasionally, in the time-honoured phrase of Howard Kirk, *The History Man*, 'against' their *institutions* (Bradbury, 1975). Corporate responses run across some familiar pathologies: not wanting to be left out; choosing the club to be associated with; reluctance to invest speculatively; and simply showing off. Thus MITx, Coursera, and Udacity (all spun off from Stanford) have now been joined by edX (Harvard and MIT). Following the trajectory set by MITOpen, costs have risen, as have expectations of designs and of the tradable value for students (credit) and investors (supplying platform services). Martin Bean, Vice-Chancellor of the Open University and chair of Futurelearn estimates that a Futurelearn MOOC, which will be designed 'for mobile first, rather than as an afterthought' will be around £30,000 (Parr, 2013).

And institutions belong to *systems* of HE: local, regional, national, national–regional and global. For some (like the California legislators presiding over the meltdown of guaranteed progression in the 'Californian Master Plan') they may be cavalry over the hill; for others (like many private-sector-dominated Boards of Governors or Trustees) they may be sticks to beat management over unit costs; for developing countries they may be part of the solution, or part of the problem of lack of resources.

The bottom line is that MOOCs are probably not (except in very peculiar circumstances) going to be a whole-system solution for anybody (student, teacher, institution, or system). They are going to be a part of the landscape for everyone, and nobody will be able to wish them away (including John Daniel, theorist of the 'mega-university', and a pioneering practitioner at Athabasca, the Open University and now the online consortium Academic Partnerships, who has declared them to be 'fatally flawed and no more than a fad' [Parr, 2013]). Meanwhile the Gates Foundation has linked up with Athabasca to launch the MOOC Research Hub to evaluate 'how they impact teaching, learning and education in general' (see website).

Developing countries could also inspire innovation and initiatives not fundamentally dependent on new technologies. Another kind of international experiment has profound moral and community service intentions. This is the Aga Khan University, established by His Highness the Aga Khan, the 49th hereditary Imam of the Shia Ismaili Muslims. Chartered in Pakistan in 1983, this remarkable institution now also has campuses in Kenya, Tanzania, Uganda, the UK, Afghanistan, Egypt, and Syria with a mission to 'promote human welfare through research, teaching and community service' (Watson *et al.*, 2011: 111–19). In his foundation address the Aga Khan referred to:

> Two fundamental aspects of our Faith: the limitlessness of God's power and the brotherhood of man. The Aga Khan University has a number of constituencies to which the Charter encourages it to respond and with which it must keep faith: the Pakistan Nation, the Islamic Ummah, including my own Community, the Third World countries of Asia and Africa.
>
> (Muborakshoeva, 2013: 107–8)

Reaching out to the wider world AKU has opened its Institute for the Study of Muslim Civilisations (ISMC) in London (Ibid. 12).

Phase 5: blurred boundaries and the 'dual sector'

Next, the latter part of the twentieth and beginning of the twenty-first centuries has seen significant action on the frontier between compulsory education, optional tertiary provision, and the initial rungs of higher education. Examples are the UK phenomenon of 'higher education in further education', the vitally important American Community College network, and the HE/TAFE 'precincts' springing up in Australia. The latest descriptor of activity in this borderland is that of 'dual sector' provision (Garrod and Macfarlane, 2009; Davis, 2010: 74). Experiments along these lines pop up in national systems with regularity, for example the German *Fachochschulen* (now renamed 'universities of applied science'). Many of them are the product of forced institutional mergers, like the new Irish 'technological universities' (an example is the consortium of the Waterford Institute of Technology and the Institute of Technology, Carlow).

Phase 6: the 'for profit' sector

The 'pattern' is rounded out by the most recent wave: that of the 'for-profits'. I want to separate these from the longer history of 'private' HE.

'Private' higher education, in the sense of major funding streams coming not from the state, has always been part of the system, and indeed the patterns set out above are largely independent of government funding until the nineteenth and twentieth centuries. Many national systems – like Poland and Japan – have had strong parallel, even majority, private sectors. Any profits (or surpluses) are normally earmarked for reinvestment in the enterprise.

The question of reputation is also very variable across different jurisdictions. In some the 'public' institutions command the highest respect (and hence levels of demand); in others it is the private. In several (such as the United States and Japan) the 'apex' institutions represent a mixture of public and private.

The global expansion of participation in higher education has predictably encouraged more strictly business interests. The tradition of 'private, not-for-profit' higher education has now been supplemented around the world by enterprises that are emphatically, 'for profit'. In many contexts this has been tolerated, or even encouraged because of a shortage of public funding. In these cases, significant commercial enterprises – in fields such as publishing, communications, or the training arms of large corporations – have seen the shareholder or dividend value that can arise from the contemporary desire for credentials. A barrier can be the regulation of awarding powers (or of institutional title) within particular jurisdictions, and this can be another of the spheres of activity within higher education where 're-regulation' of an unsatisfactory outcome proves much more difficult than the enabling relaxation or deregulation.

At the time of writing the UK system is anxiously watching the outcome of the sale of one of its only four for-profit enterprises, the College of Law – its degree-awarding powers having been granted on the recommendation of the regulator (the Quality Assurance Agency for Higher Education [QAA]) – to a private equity firm, with its (admittedly time-limited) accreditation intact (see Morgan, 2102a). In November 2012 the College duly earned university status (the first private institution to do so since the University of Buckingham in 1983) as the for-profit University of Law (Morgan, 2012b). At the same time a major publisher, Pearson (owner of both the *Financial Times* and the Examination Board Edexcel) has entered the field by setting up Pearson College, with awards validated by Royal Holloway and Bedford College (see website).

Meanwhile the US experience of public money being accessed by students on courses in for-profit institutions has led to widespread concerns, including at the political level. A Senate Committee chaired by Senator Tom Harkin in July 2012 raised questions about: the rates of non-completion (over 50 per cent); the balance of resources expended on recruitment, profit-taking, and instruction (22, 19 and 17 per cent respectively); and the high rates of loan finance (96 per cent of all students holding loans, compared with 57 per cent at four-year private colleges, 48 per cent at four-year public colleges, and 13 per cent at community colleges) (Stratford, 2012). To check on a familiar barometer of the American public mood, the issue has even made the 'Doonesbury' cartoon series, as President King of Walden College looks at these numbers and considers going 'for profit', including for the effect on his salary (Holdaway, 2012).

Collectively the 'for-profits' are pursuing several markets. One is simply mass enrolment, going back to the mega-universities of phase four. The University of Phoenix peaked at 600,000 students worldwide in 2010 (Barber *et al.*, 2013: 18). Anhanguera, the 'largest for-profit learning network in Brazil, is valued at US$1.4 billion, claims to be second in size only to the Apollo group, and serves hundreds of thousands of students through (currently) 67 campuses and 650 training centres (see website). Others, and sometimes other parts of the same holding companies, are going for the higher value professional niches (such as law and business), where their infrastructure costs are likely to be lower than in conventional universities operating across a full subject range. Another insufficiently explored issue is how far they need to rely on the traditional sector for 'moonlighting' staff.

My basic argument is that this pattern of six layers constitutes a robust, empirical shape for university foundations all around the world. Different societies, and their national systems, can be shown to join in at various points, but they generally follow the same sequence of events from the point when they do so. The UK, much of Europe, and the United States (through the colonial seminaries – between Harvard [1636], Yale [1701] and Princeton [1746]), can claim to have been there from the beginning. Latin America was in step, with religiously inspired foundations such as San Marcos (Lima, Peru) in 1551, Córdoba (Argentina) in 1613, and San Carlos (Guatemala) in 1676. Several currently developed economies can claim to join in phase two: for example, Australia with its 'sandstone' universities (Sydney in 1850 and Melbourne in 1853), followed by New Zealand (Otago in 1869 and Auckland in 1883), as well as the Imperial Universities of Japan (like Tokyo in 1867) and China (for example, Peking in 1898). At this stage (and in the next), the process of joining in could lead to suppression of alternative, indigenous higher education traditions. For example, this is Muborakshovea's verdict on the fate of the rich late medieval Islamic tradition (discussed further in Chapter 2 below):

> The whole of educational developments in the nineteenth- to early twentieth-century Muslim contexts largely fit this pattern of *transition* from indigenous to European models, *formation* of new institutions and

exercising *innovation* in the process. ... Thus the conceptualisation of universities in Muslim contexts since the nineteenth century has been closely connected with the political, ideological and security concerns of colonialists, Muslim monarchs and the state.

(Muborakshoeva, 2013: 45–6)

Many other societies, including those with 'colonial' and 'independence' heritage, first experienced the 'publicly planned' approach of phase three (Ghana in 1948, Indonesia in 1947, Ceylon in 1942, the West Indies in 1948, and so on). The 'innovations' of phase four spring up all over the world, particularly in societies with ambitions for rapid growth (like the mega-universities of the sub-continent and parts of Asia), but also in 'developed' contexts. The 'blurred boundaries' of phase five emerge around the turn of the present century, partly as a legacy of the 'binary' thinking referred to above, partly as an attempt to 'democratize' tertiary education, and partly as a recognition that alternative routes for post-compulsory education increasingly need to be planned and delivered together. The newcomer (the 'for-profit' approach of phase six) is significantly dependent on a favourable regulatory environment. There is also evidence that it works best when the relevant private bodies are able to work in partnership with established (including publicly funded) institutions. Like several of the innovative approaches of phase four, it also has a distinct global reach.

Contending narratives, capitals, and pedagogies

The narrative history of universities is capable of sustaining several 'Whig' theories, encapsulating contending views of progress and development towards a preferred vision of the present. Another approach, by Linda Colley (following Roger Smith) calls such long narrative sweeps 'constitutive stories ... that recount the key historical events that formed a community' and 'the "priceless" character traits that community members have evolved as a result' (Colley, 2012).

In terms of universities' self-image, these have clustered around four nodes:

1. The *liberal* theory of higher education as self-realization and social transformation, including latterly an element of social mobility and meritocracy that perhaps reaches its height (and certainly retains its most important talisman) in Cardinal Newman.
2. The professional formation theory. This identifies universities and colleges as providers of expertise in some areas that have been continuous (law, medicine, and theology) and some that are relatively new (engineering, science, and public administration).
3. Higher education can be seen as a *research engine*, allied to regional and national ambitions for economic growth. In this area contemporary governments have rediscovered, rather than invented, priorities that were high over a century ago.

Variations on this theme include higher education as a source of *business services*, and of *national pride*.

4. Finally, there is the relatively recently rediscovered seam of *civic and community engagement*, which is almost invariably present at the creation of the other narratives set out above, but sometimes suppressed in their interests (Watson, 2007).

Each of these narratives (or theories) can, of course, be recast in a dysfunctional or negative light. The liberal aspiration can become a means of social selection and exclusion. Aggressively individualistic notions of advancement can lead to discrimination. Professionalism can lead to narrow and self-interested instrumentalism. Research can ignore some of its wider ethical responsibilities, and national pride can convert into short-term state priorities. And so on.

Another way of formulating the narrative is in terms of the type of 'capital' the enterprise is intended to create.

At its heart the university is a reservoir of intellectual capital: its most fundamental purpose is about the creation, testing, and application of knowledge. As a consequence the twenty-first century preoccupation with knowledge management ought to be highly congenial to the higher education enterprise. To probe this further, it is helpful to assess the types of intellectual capital apparently preferred (and potentially privileged) in the wider society.

This section updates and develops the analysis in my *Managing Civic and Community Engagement* (Watson, 2007: 14–17). It focuses on a number of features of competing concepts of capital, and the role of higher education in delivering them. These include: the 'mode of production' each assumes is most important in securing economic and other objectives; the chief values each implies; the performance indicators on which each relies to measure progress; the key practical outcomes each anticipates; and perhaps most revealingly the forms of trust or mutuality involved in each case (on the latter, see Smith, 2005).

Traditionally the battle lines have been drawn between an economically focused preoccupation with human capital, seeing qualified manpower as an essential element of growth, and a community-focused desire for enhanced social capital, seeing education at all levels as a way of solidifying cohesive norms of mutually satisfying behaviour.

Human capital is fundamentally an economic concept, associated with the work of Gary Becker in particular (see Schuller, 1998). It is fundamentally aimed at understanding how skills and a trained workforce can add value. It proceeds largely by aggregating the assets accumulated by individuals, either through qualifications or the duration of the educational experience. The main outcome towards which it is directed is increased productivity and national or regional economic 'edge'. In so far as it is about a form of trust, it emphasizes calculation and predictability: the kind of trust you would hope to have in your bank.

Social capital is most frequently traced back to the work of Robert Putnam, although this has now invited a critique based on how poorly it deals with difference and 'otherness'. It has attracted interest and admiration all over the world for what it appears to say about the power and resilience of communities. It focuses on networked relationships and their shared norms and values, rather than on qualified individuals. The key values that emerge are in terms of developing mutual obligations and a strengthened sense of civil society. The trust appealed to here is one closer to membership than contract. For this reason it deals less well with opposition, otherness, and difference, and much of its initial promise has dissolved in the face of the problems not just of divided societies, but also cultural diversity. This defect is becoming more and more apparent, as set out in the following critique:

> The basic lesson that emerges from Putnam's research is that high levels
> of diversity currently have a negative impact on levels of social capital …
> Relative to a more homogenous community, Putnam's research concludes
> that greater diversity means that a community will exhibit less trust,
> sociability, political participation and interclass mixing. Social capital, it
> would seem, thrives in places where 'diversity' has been effaced.
>
> (Hallberg and Lund, 2005; see also Bartlett, 2012)

A relatively new kid on the block is the theory of *creative* capital, associated in particular with the work of Richard Florida (Florida, 2002). It tackles the issues of difference and otherness head on. It has proved much more persuasive at the local (including metropolitan) levels than when scaled up to regions, nations, or global regions. Here the focus is on voluntary associations and 'clusters' of like-minded or similarly motivated people: the 'super-creative core' of Florida's more general 'creative class' of brain-workers. Tolerant and diverse host communities seem essential; there is a premium on bohemianism and gay-friendliness. Formal entry barriers are more or less non-existent; it is what you can do and how innovative your ideas are that counts, not what qualifications you have. Innovation is the goal, and fluid experimentation the key. Fluidity also applies to the communities themselves; they will dissolve and form at will. As a consequence the type of trust on which they depend is personal, direct, and highly affective.

Yet another recent invention is *identity* capital (Côté, 2002) – comprising the attributes individuals need to 'intelligently strategize and make decisions affecting their life courses' (this one can easily degrade into Bourdieu's concept of 'symbolic capital' – shared by a self-perpetuating elite). It begins with the individual, but in this case is ultimately not about aggregate economic impact as much as individual life-courses. The drive is towards self-reliance, self-confidence, and self-efficacy. What works for one individual may not work for another, but the goal is a personal story, based upon sound and informed decision-making, and an ultimate trust in the individual to get it right, eventually.

Governments have also begun to get involved, for example through the British government's 'foresight' exercise on '*mental* capital and wellbeing' (Beddington *et al.*, 2008). As an 'official' formulation, it is interested in the twin goals of economic competitiveness and social cohesion; it is about prosperity and peace. In this sense the goal is to ensure that members of the society can contribute productively and happily. Mental health and its reciprocal, mental incapacity, are thus critical. Perhaps understandably, the key inputs are seen as public policy-related, and the trust sought is that elected representatives and other authorities will do the right thing.

Finally, the ex-British Prime Minister Tony Blair has promoted '*spiritual* capital' as the core concept for his new interfaith foundation (Blair, 2008). It will be attractive to those who see revealed religion in particular as the source of appropriate behaviour. It will also have resonance for those with a non-dogmatic ethical approach. However, in the hands of Blair and others it quickly reduces to a bland confidence in interfaith harmony. His analysis is all about the old-fashioned merits of understanding the other point of view – provided it is brigaded within the disciplines of organized religion, and structured around common denominators like the golden mean or the Kantian categorical imperative. The trust is that knowing more about the other will reduce tension and spread sweetness and light.

Other more marginal contenders include 'capital capital' (as in Olympics venues, see *The Economist*, 2012a), 'adventure capital' (see *Conserving Lakeland*, 2012), 'natural capital' (or maintenance of 'the ecosystems … [that are] essential to human wellbeing and sustainable development' – see the 'natural capital' website), and (notoriously) Catherine Hakim's 'erotic capital' (Hakim, 2011).

They may sound abstract, but these theoretical models matter. They represent a way of capturing priorities for the higher education enterprise that will have resonance for governments, for communities, and for the members of universities and colleges. To put it crudely in terms of their major emphases, though of course these interests overlap: governments want human capital; communities want both this and the cohesive capital associated with social capital; modern students and their teachers, however, are increasingly interested in creativity and breaking the mould.

Teachers and those designing the educational experience of students will adopt, adapt, and blend specific pedagogical approaches and techniques to bring about the desired results. Talking about teaching in the modern academy can be something of a hit and miss affair. At one end of the scales are all of the initiatives to improve the student experience (especially in a context of increasing awareness about personal cost and investment); the drive to have higher education teachers professionally qualified (as in the UK's adoption through the Higher Education Academy [HEA] of 'professional standards' [HEA, 2011]); the efflorescence of teaching awards at institutional and at national level; the development of specialist units; the assignment of responsibility for teaching matters to senior posts at university, faculty and departmental level; the ubiquity of annual teaching and learning conferences; the emergence of specialist journals; the adoption of feedback and student satisfaction surveys; and the political drive for accountability for quality and intensity of teaching inputs and so on (see Bamber *et al.*, 2009 for an overview). At the other end of the scales there is the growing, almost defeatist, claim that careers, institutional reputation, and above all success in access to competitive funding, is all that counts; that in the UK case the periodic audits of research volume, quality, impact, and environment are (in the words of a former government chief adviser) 'the only game in town' (Watson 2011).

There is an irony here, in that as Steve Fuller and others have argued, both the historical origins and much of the modern development of the university (the 'layers' above) have had as a priority instruction, education more widely, and the professional development of students. Research has been a means to the end of teaching more frequently than the reverse. In Fuller's words:

> I believe that the university is a social technology for manufacturing knowledge as a public good. This goal is most clearly realized the more that research – which is always in the first instance novel and hence esoteric – is translated into teaching, and hence made available to people who had nothing to do with its original production and are likely to take that knowledge in directions other than those intended, or even desired, by the original researchers. This feat of epistemic justice is most obviously performed in the construction of curricular materials like course outlines, textbooks and other pedagogical devices.
>
> (Basbøll and Fuller, 2008)

Lee Shulman, President of the Carnegie Foundation for the Advancement of Teaching, has developed the powerful concept of the 'signature pedagogy' to examine how the professions look at the 'challenge of teaching people to understand, to act, and to be integrated into a complex way of knowing, doing, and being'. Examples are the clinical ward round, the law school case conference, the engineering project, the priestly apprenticeship, and so on (Shulman, 2005). This can, I believe, be expanded to cover the primary goals of whole higher education institutions in differing eras and contexts. Broadly, seven major pedagogical styles and techniques can be separated. As with many of the taxonomies presented in this book, they can flex and overlap between each other.

The first (including chronologically) has to be *dogmatic instruction*. This is fundamentally organized around a holy book or books and the associated commentary and exegesis. The modal inspiration is perhaps the educational parts of the sixth century 'Rule of St Benedict', based as it is on humility and 'unhesitating obedience'. The curriculum is 'holy reading' and 'prayer', and during Lent each monk 'is to receive a book from the Library, and is to read the whole of it straight through' (Fry, 1982: 28, 29, 70). Later on such discipline could be adapted as a style for secular purposes, as in Marxist-Leninist orthodoxy, or even some curricula developed in the wake of proclaimed scholarly prophets or leaders. Most contemporary institutions with a religious dogmatic intent (for example, the *madrasas* of the sub-continent) are, however, now regarded as outside the family of higher education.

The second was also present almost at the creation of the modern university and leads to membership of an expert group or profession (whether or not they act as Adam Smith's 'conspiracy against the public'). In the modern era this leads to *expert credentialism*, as in the 'licence to practise' or to charge for services. The contemporary guardians of this arena are generally outside the academy, in the Professional and Statutory bodies (see, for example, the website for the framework of European Standards for degrees in Nursing). A familiar teaching tool is the use of case studies – or simulations of decision-making or action in the 'real' world.

Meanwhile, as an essential part of the liberal, emancipatory theory of higher education, a pedagogical style develops that could be called individual *self-discovery*. The goal here is for the individual learner to achieve an independent point of view, and a personal voice. Ron Barnett captures the letting go, or the 'leap' that this implies in his *A Will to Learn*: 'The *pedagogical challenge* [emphasis in the original] lies in the student's will being so formed that she wills herself to go forward into those spaces which may challenge her being itself' (Barnett, 2007: 155).

For a long time the key here lay in close personal reading: of the classics (religious and secular), of 'great books' in general, and the construction of both canons of literature and idiosyncratic interdisciplinary collections of study like Oxford's Philosophy, Politics, and Economics (PPE) – soon to be challenged as an *ensemble*, by the new Blavatnik School of Government's Masters degree in Public Policy (MPP, see website). In the USA the inspirational equivalent is the Harvard 'core' – a pattern of requirements that has been constantly tinkered with and overhauled in the modern era (Watson, 2007: 142–4).

The Socratic method and the fetishization of the 'tutorial' method play their part regularly (Palfreyman, 2008; Madden, 2012). Oxford, which has built a promotional strategy around one-to-one (or at least very small group) teaching, directed by senior scholars, finds it hard to acknowledge that this is by no means uniformly delivered, including to undergraduates. Meanwhile, historically, it is equally unpalatable to have to acknowledge that the modern system began as a form of cramming – by private tutors, usually away from the College – to get not very bright middle and upper-class students through examinations, including for the Indian Civil Service. To be irresponsibly anachronistic, at its point of modern reinvention it was a species of 'dumbing down' (Harvie, 1976: 54–9). What really seems to count for students in this pedagogical context is personal feedback on written and other work, especially in the context of formative assessment. This is something around which the Open University has structured both its teacher-training and its learning strategy, even though the communication is technologically mediated and there isn't an armchair or a glass of sherry in sight. It may also partly explain why the OU does so well on key aspects of student satisfaction recorded in the UK's National Student Survey (NSS).

A more programmatic form of external engagement reaches its height in the North American enthusiasm for *service learning*, or using the resources of the surrounding community for learning scenarios (McIlrath and Mac Labhrainn, 2007: 65–82; 103–70). At one end of the spectrum lies volunteering (whether or not on the basis of expertise), including for course credit; at the other lies the educational goal of deep but temporary immersion in the dilemmas of particular groups in civil society.

Service-learning can, however, be less structured than another well-established approach to Deweyite 'learning by doing'. The *Practicum* has a long and honourable tradition in professional higher education in particular, often involving supervised but 'live' practice, and sometimes overlapping with periods of probationary service, after graduation but before full qualification. 'Sandwich' courses, with periods in industry, and what is called in the USA 'cooperative learning' play a distinctive part here. As for the pedagogical approaches involved, perhaps the best contemporary definition comes from Guy Claxton and his colleagues at the University of Winchester's Centre for Real-World Learning (prepared for the City & Guilds Institute):

> The evidence is clear that vocational education needs to be taught in the context of practical problem-solving. The best vocational learning is broadly hands-on, practical, experiential, real-world as well as, and often at the same time as, something which involves feedback, questioning, application and reflection, and, when required, theoretical models and explanations. The research identifies a number of tried and tested teaching methods including learning by watching, imitating, practicing (trial and error), through feedback, through conversation, by teaching and helping, by real-world problem solving, through enquiry, by thinking critically and producing knowledge, by listening, transcribing and remembering, by drafting and sketching, by reflecting, on the fly, by being coached, by competing, through virtual environments, through simulation and role-play, and through games.
>
> (Lucas, *et al.*, 2012: 4)

Some would say that John Dewey is alive and well.

Each of these so far incorporates a mix of methods of inquiry, which can often be elevated to the level of *research apprenticeship*, whether in the core techniques of the sciences, social sciences, or arts and humanities.

Finally, for many, especially in the modern world, 'graduation' is not the sole target, or the final outcome. Post-compulsory education and training has become a much more flexible and messy affair, achieving its goals for many through complex patterns of *lifelong learning*. Here qualifications and part-qualifications need not be sequential or connected, in subject or level. They can be chosen, or prescribed for tactical, strategic or entirely serendipitous reasons (Schuller and Watson, 2009).

Taking the pedagogical choices in the longer view, there are some overarching themes at work. One is the rise of co-creation and co-design (a feature of the 'conversation' discussed in Chapter 6 below). Another is the way in which the debate has moved from teaching to learning support, and the kind of integrated approach this requires from the deployment of institutional resources. For example, the 'student experience' and 'learning support' are two of the three examples Celia Whitchurch gives in her thesis about the emergence of 'third space professionals' (broadly bridging academic and administrative backgrounds); the third is 'community and business partnership' (Whitchurch, 2013: 25).

Curricular dystopians regularly bewail what university students can't do that their predecessors (by which they normally mean themselves) did with ease. Ron Dearing – the author of manifold reviews across the age range in the UK – once called this the 'twenty-year' problem: today it's awful, twenty years ago it was all right; except that twenty years ago it was also seen as awful and nothing like as good as forty years ago; and so on (Dearing, 1996: 6). Sometimes the more positive voices get a reality check, as in Mary Beard's comparison of the Classics Tripos in Cambridge of 1900 and 2000. It is genuinely harder now:

> Well, put aside any romantic nostalgia for the glory days of rigorous classical education at the turn of the nineteenth and twentieth centuries. The good news is that what our undergraduates face at the beginning of the twenty-first is actually rather more challenging. ... You certainly had to *know* a lot. But there isn't a lot of evidence that a lot of *thinking* was required. ... The question from last year's paper 'What role did religion play in policing sexual practice?' would have floored most of the class of 1901/02 for more than the obvious reasons.
>
> (Beard, 2009: 78–9)

At one end of the co-creation spectrum are the opportunities simply for students to decide themselves what it is they want to learn; their teachers have to agree on how it will be assessed. This led to the 'independent study' movement in the UK in the late 1970s and early 1980s (pioneers were The University of Lancaster, North East London Polytechnic, and Oxford Polytechnic [Pratt, 1997: 151–2; Watson, 1989: 29–31]). This process is satirized effectively in Steve Pink's *American Pie*-style movie *Accepted* (2006) in which a group of high school seniors, disappointing their parents by failing to get into college anywhere, create their own (the South Harmon Institute of Technology – I shall not include the acronym), initially online and then for real in a disused mental hospital. They get away with it for a while. They write their own curriculum – on a wall – and one of the highlights is when this is wheeled into a meeting of the State Board of Accreditation. At the other end is the drive by almost all courses leading to licence to practise (at both first and second cycle levels) to create 'researching professionals', capable not only of assessing cues to evidence-based practice, but also of carrying out their own investigations. In between are all the cases where students are ahead of the classroom game (notably in terms of ICT), discussed further below in the context of generational tensions (Chapter 6). In Keri Facer's words we have to get beyond the retrospective 'banking' theory of knowledge and skills:

> We need to create educational relationships where teachers, parents, children and grandparents can come together as 'co-conspirators' to learn from and collaborate with each other. We need to create institutions that enable people of different generations to learn together to understand and to overcome those challenges that are of common concern to us all. In so doing, we will begin to create the relationships and institutions that can underpin a multi-generational conversation about the future.
>
> (Facer, 2011: 40–1)

The long story is that, in general, the contemporary claim that better teaching and better course design involves students more in what is being learned, how it is being learned, and what the most effective means of assessing that it has been learned are, has progressively and at least partially been justified.

The resulting intentions – captured by these narratives, capitals, and pedagogies – matter: to leaders and members of universities and to those who attempt to steer them from outside, including governments, funders, and public opinion more generally. Collectively they cover several 'purposes' for initial higher education, which are sometimes mutually reinforcing, but more often in conflict.

University 'purposes': Ten claims

Louis Menand has recently (and in a similar spirit of 'owning up' – his article is entitled 'Live and Learn: Why we have college') reduced these to three competing claims for contemporary higher education.

His 'Theory 1' is that higher education is a product of meritocracy: 'College is, essentially a four-year intelligence test'. One of its main 'services' is that it 'sorts people according to ability'. Such sorting aims to replace the outcomes of an earlier elite system that was 'largely in the business of reproducing a privileged social class'. 'Theory 2' is more aspirational and fundamentally 'democratic'. 'College exposes future citizens to material that enlightens and empowers them, whatever careers they end up choosing.' 'Theory 3' brings in the vocational element: 'as work becomes more high tech, employers demand more people with specialized training'. This links with the growth of second-cycle higher education: '[m]aking college a prerequisite for professional school was probably the most important reform ever made in American higher education'. None of these theories work, however, without student effort, and no such effect is simply purchased. 'College was *supposed* to be hard. Its difficulty was a token of its transformational powers' (Menand, 2011).

Without contradicting Menand's big three, the analysis in this book spreads longer and wider, encompassing at least ten separable sets of purposes:

The first is *religious,* and acknowledges the role of higher education in confirming faith, and from time to time inspiring it, as through conversion. Doctrinal (and even dogmatic) instruction is central.

The second is about *personal development,* with a string of evocative descriptors: self-realization, self-discovery, self-creation, and so on. It links with a discourse about establishing the authenticity of the individual actor. Pedagogically the key is independent learning.

The third is more *social,* looking at ways in which the individual improves his or her relationship with a wider world: culturally, economically, politically, and so on. It can end up in a form of education for citizenship (including world citizenship). It also incorporates more local pedagogies, such as service learning.

The fourth is about *technical know-how,* where higher education (often in combination with outside forms of recognition) essentially attests the ability of the graduate to be able to perform certain functions at specified levels.

The fifth links with this but incorporates the wider question of *professional acculturation.* 'Membership' of a profession thus aligns with membership of the university.

The sixth emphasizes the relationship of the student to his or her peers, whether or not this is structured through an intended profession. Much of the longer-term effects of higher education are claimed to be through *networks,* established or discovered at university and relied upon for the remainder of careers or even the rest of life.

The seventh focuses on accelerated *maturation,* or time and space to 'grow up'. It is seen as connected with moving away from home (although for many part-time and an increasing number of full-time students) this doesn't formally apply.

An eighth draws upon the notion of *protected time,* stressing that higher education is potentially an 'interval' on the career-driven part of the life-course. Again it will not apply in the same way to students on some professional courses, or to many part-timers (who are 'learning and earning' and for whom credentials are critical).

The ninth is about subjects and disciplines, independent of their professional or applied settings. Many students are drawn to higher education by an inspiring teacher at secondary level or by '*love of the subject*'. Once in – and beyond – their institutional experience they then get empanelled in campaigns to protect or promote 'their' subject.

The final strand is best summed up perhaps as *mental gymnastics*. There are claims that higher education is more demanding than that which precedes it, and in many cases follows it. As Menand says, 'College was *supposed* to be hard'. There's also the touch of the Tiger Mother at work here. Amy Chua famously stated that 'what Chinese parents understand is that nothing is fun until you are good at it' (Yu, 2011). The *Financial Times* columnist Lucy Kellaway seems, as usual, to have hit the nail on the head. 'Nothing you do in your working lives', she reassures her daughters preparing for exams 'will ever be as bad as this': 'GCSEs, A-Levels and finals are a hell that nothing in the office will ever match'. But, in a curious way, they will be worth it:

> Even though I've forgotten what I learnt, I am still proud to have once known it. This seems a less shameful state of ignorance than never having known it at all ... exams demand clarity of thought and expression and penalise waffle and bullshit. Whereas in business, alas, waffle and bullshit have become the gold standard.

> (Kellaway, 2009)

This, like all of the elements on this list, is at least contested, not least by those who think that things will never be as hard as when they were at university themselves.

Put together, there are several claims here about the role of higher education: in existential terms (how participants come to be); in epistemological terms (how they think and appraise information); in behavioural terms (how they learn to conduct themselves); and in positional terms (including through competition and collaboration). Some are open (and provisional); some are closed (and create compliance). Some (in the words of Donald Kennedy) are about 'leadership' and others about 'lag' (Kennedy, 1997: 265).

The validity and the applicability of such claims will vary over time, by institutional setting, by subject and mode of study, according to the expectations of funders and other stakeholders, and critically in terms of the approach taken by the student himself or herself. Another way of looking at them is as a menu of possibilities across which differing styles of presentation and choice can be played: 'plat du jour', 'à la carte', or 'smörgåsbord'.

The remainder of this work attempts to see where such claims come from, how much contemporary resonance any of them still have, and above all whether or not they can combine to create a moral compass (a form of personal responsibility). It is structured around five sets of questions. In philosophical terms these are part-ethical (what higher education should be seeking to inspire or inculcate in terms of habits of thinking) and part-epistemological (how it proceeds to validate certain types of knowledge):

- *The Question of Conscience (especially through religious foundations).*
- *The Question of Character (as formed through 'liberal' higher education).*

- *The Questions of Calling, Competence, and Craft (in the zones of professional and vocational higher education).*
- *The Question of Citizenship (as in respective obligations to civil society, the state and global responsibilities).*
- *The Question of Capability (the role of higher education in inculcating life-skills, including employability).*

Chapter 2

The question of conscience

This chapter explores one of the earliest and most enduringly influential 'layers' of university purposes: that of maintaining, enhancing and subjecting to supportive criticism the goal of ethical – especially doctrinal – instruction.

Defending the faith

I need to begin this chapter with a disclaimer. The geological layers identified in the last chapter relate to the origins and development of the modern (by which I mean post-thirteenth-century) European University. There was another start, highly significant in any comprehensive account of the world history of the university, and subject to at least some of the same initial dilemmas of marrying (or not) the strands of religious, scientific (including philosophical), and professional knowledge.

This was the Islamic university, beginning under the caliphates of the Middle East and North Africa in the tenth and eleventh centuries, reaching its heights and stimulating the later (post-1500) development of higher education traditions in both Iran and India, before going into decline in the twelfth and thirteenth centuries. In this formative period the Islamic system not only sought to absorb Greek thought, but produced its intellectual heroes in Avicenna (980–1037) and Averroes (1126–98). Marodsilton Muborakshoeva has recently produced an excellent overview of this story, this phase of which she characterizes as follows:

> [T]he intellectual engagement with and debates on issues and concerns important for Muslim communities led to the formulation of a world-view with a pluralistic concept of knowledge and epistemology, and yet within the all-embracing framework of revelation.
>
> (Muborakshoeva, 2013: 19)

In the main part of her book (*Islam and Higher Education*) Muborakshoeva proceeds to set these historical commitments in the context of modern universities in Islamic jurisdictions (notably Pakistan). 'Conscience' tunes initially with religious purposes, and can shade into dogmatic instruction. This was the main outcome of the Islamic tradition as it streamed into the worlds of mosques and madrasas. In Muborakshoeva's words:

> Now modern higher education mainly prepares individuals without religious, cultural and civilizational knowledge, whereas the indigenous madrasahs' functions and roles have been reduced to preparing religious

leaders, Shari'a lawyers and some language teachers, as compared with the broad choice of jobs they enjoyed before.

(Ibid. 23, 28)

Meanwhile in its European origins the university had more general purposes. Here are two examples: one of a College founded by an aristocratic patron; the other the result of a papal bull. Together with the development of cathedral schools these were the dominant modes of higher education foundation.

The first is Elizabeth de Burgh (Lady Clare), who founded Clare College in 1359, setting out a 'mission statement':

> Through their study and teaching at the University the scholars should discover and acquire the precious pearl of learning so that it does not stay hidden under a bushel but is displayed abroad to enlighten those who walk in the dark paths of ignorance.

(Shaw-Miller, 2001)

The second is the Papal Bull of Innocent VIII establishing the University of Aberdeen in 1495:

> In the northern parts of the kingdom the people are ignorant and almost barbarous owing to their distance from a university. The city is near these places and suitable for a university, where all lawful faculties could be taught to both ecclesiastics and laymen, who would thus acquire the most precious pearl of knowledge, and so promote the well-being of the kingdom and the salvation of souls.

(University of Aberdeen, 1906)

The 'pearl' is a particularly evocative metaphor, and draws upon a rich seam of medieval allegory (notably in the work of the fourteenth-century 'Pearl poet', who was probably also the author of *Sir Gawain and the Green Knight*.) It requires grit to get it started: it is created in a relatively sealed environment, but it only achieves a real value once it leaves that protected environment. What's more, that value can be of various kinds: aesthetic and symbolic, as well as a tradable commodity. There is much more poetry here than in the concept of the 'third leg' (or 'arm' or 'mission').

At this stage the academic mode of production was structured around scholasticism, the mode of Biblical and related criticism derived from St Thomas Aquinas. As a 'layer', even this survives today. My Green Templeton and Oxford colleague Richard Pring, professor emeritus of education, writes about his experience as a student in the 1950s of the Venerable English College of Rome, which was founded in 1579 and is still flourishing (see website). The first three years of the course (designed, along seminary lines, as a preparation for the priesthood) were dedicated to philosophy studied on the principles of syllogistic thinking, or scholasticism. He includes this wonderfully evocative diary entry:

> There was an argument: can sleep be enjoyed? Pro: since one looks forward to it so much, although one is intimately acquainted with it over many years, it must be enjoyed. Con: since one is in a state of unconsciousness during sleep, one cannot enjoy it. A dilemma, and this is what we argued about in Castel Sant'Angelo gardens.
>
> (Pring, 2008: 187)

However, from the fifteenth and sixteenth century the European Renaissance and humanism challenged the establishment while the Continental, English, and American Reformations made their mark on this tradition, opening up the possibility of more personal readings of the Bible. In 1611 the translators of the King James or Authorized Version translated the description of a scholar in the Book of Ecclesiasticus as follows:

> The wisdom of a learned man cometh by opportunity of leisure: and he that hath little business shall become wise. But he that giveth his mind to the law of the most High, and is occupied in the meditation thereof, will seek out the wisdom of all the ancient, and be occupied in prophecies.
>
> He will keep the sayings of the renowned men: and where subtil parables are, he will be there also.
>
> He will seek out the secrets of grave sentences, and be conversant in dark parables.
>
> He shall serve among great men, and appear before princes: he will travel through strange countries; for he hath tried the good and the evil among men.
>
> He will give his heart to resort early to the Lord that made him, and will pray before the most High, and will open his mouth in prayer, and make supplication for his sins.
>
> When the great Lord will, he shall be filled with the spirit of understanding: he shall pour out wise sentences, and give thanks unto the Lord in his prayer.
>
> He shall direct his counsel and knowledge, and in his secrets shall he meditate.
>
> He shall shew forth that which he hath learned, and shall glory in the law of the covenant of the Lord.

Many shall commend his understanding; and so long as the world endureth, it shall not be blotted out; his memorial shall not depart away, and his name shall live from generation to generation.

Nations shall shew forth his wisdom, and the congregation shall declare his praise.

If he die, he shall leave a greater name than a thousand: and if he live, he shall increase it.

(*Ecclesiaticus*, 38: 24; 39: 1–11)

There is, in some senses, a striking modernity about this manifesto. It includes the autonomy of the scholar, the method of close reading, the way he is in demand around the world, and the guarantee of a permanent reputation for excellence. In May 2012 the pan-European Union student mobility scheme named after Erasmus of Rotterdam celebrated its 25th anniversary. Desiderius Erasmus (1466 or 1469–1536), the quintessential early-modern peripatetic humanist, had at various times been a student and a teacher at the universities of Paris, Leuven, Basel, Oxford, and Cambridge (Levi, 1971: 32–43). British participation in his scheme reached in 2012 a record 13,000 students, mostly from the more prosperous institutions. However, this represented less than two per cent of the total of 300,000 compared with over ten per cent from each of France, Germany, and Spain (Grove, 2012). And the pace is hotting up: the Leuven Ministerial Meeting of 2099 set a target of 20 per cent participation across the European Community by 2020 (Sweeney, 2013: 10–11).

In the seventeenth century however, all of this was in the context of direct revelation and doctrinal orthodoxy. At about the same time a similar trajectory was being followed by the American colonial seminaries, many of which subsequently became not only research universities but also expensive private schools in the United States, including the heart of the Ivy League. In 1643 a pamphlet called 'New England's First Fruits' explained the mission of Harvard College as follows:

To advance *learning* and perpetuate it to posterity; dreading to leave an illiterate Ministry to the Churches, when our present Ministers shall lie in the dust.

(Reuben in Kiss and Euben, 2007: 27)

Judith Reuben reminds us that 'Harvard was created not just to save souls, but to sustain a righteous community', and Robert Alter that Hebrew was a required language for all first year students in the new College in 1636 (Alter, 2010: 2). Delbanco suggests that some of this pedagogical purpose survives in the concept of 'grace': 'Every true teacher, after all, understands that along with teacher and students, a mysterious third force is present in every classroom'. He unpacks the core social purpose:

> We tend not to remember, or perhaps deliberately to forget, that college was once conceived not as a road to wealth or as a screening device for a social club, but as a training ground for pastors, teachers, and, more broadly, public servants.
>
> (Delbanco, 2012: 48, 65)

At this stage in university and college history the question of 'otherness' hardly arose. It did so, with a vengeance, however, as the initially exclusive religious communities transformed themselves into social enclaves, by, for example, establishing initially formal, later necessarily informal (for legal reasons) discrimination against groups like Jews and Asians (Karabel, 2005; Golden, 2007). Meanwhile, as some seminaries have become 'stuck' in their doctrinal allegiances, most of the Ivy League has shifted its priorities towards competing as contemporary research-led international universities. (The geological 'pipes' referred to in Chapter 1 have, however, sometimes proved robust; it was only in 1964 that Princeton excused its freshmen from compulsory attendance at chapel.)

'Otherness' bites in another way. Conscience-based academic communities can express confirmatory, majoritarian endorsement of community norms. They can also be the rock in the stream around which opposition and alternatives can gather. 'Sects' as well as 'churches' have been good at creating and using colleges, not least in North America. For an example of a recent Islamic seminary, in the American heartland, see the foundation (in 2009) and mission of Zaytuna College in Berkeley California:

> By aspiring to produce scholars who understand the specific needs of contemporary societies, we believe Zaytuna College has an important contribution to make in the indigenization of Islam in the West. An indigenized Islam is of particular significance at this time when there is so much suspicion directed toward Muslims as illegitimate 'outsiders', while at the same time a demonstrated desire on the part of many in the West, especially in America, to create a more open, multicultural, and tolerant society.
>
> (see website)

'Many faiths and none'

In contemporary terms specifically religious higher education institutions have fallen back on an argument based on *ethos*. Spiritual people will feel comfortable as members, from 'many faiths or none' (Furlong, 2013: 62). University of Melbourne Vice-Chancellor Glyn Davis describes the modern public university as 'secular and non-partisan, welcoming all creeds and none' (Davis, 2010: 42).

The secularism can be backgrounded. This, for example, is how the fifteen members of the UK's 'Cathedrals Group' of higher education institutions claim distinctiveness: 'We are the only grouping in the higher education landscape overtly based on ethical beliefs and values' (Wooldridge and Newcomb, 2011: 9). Interestingly, they have both a common history and a current dependence on teacher education. In 2011 they commissioned an external report on their strategic positioning 'in an otherwise secular and increasingly market driven sector'. The authors concluded as follows:

> The faith-based institutions are rising to the challenge of being successful 21st century universities and university colleges whilst seeking to retain their core values and ethos: all are welcoming to students 'of all faiths or none' and it is particularly striking that Muslim students and their parents are happy to favour faith-based institutions where they know that faith is valued and respected. As part of the adaptation process, many in the Group have developed links with institutions with other histories and cultures, some purely secular. Such embracing of a 'wider' or 'no faith' position has taken place without undermining the Christian heritage. This flexibility of purpose allied to tenaciously sustaining core values should prove to be a great strength in the difficult times ahead.
>
> (Ibid. 4)

More generally, the Higher Education Funding Council for England (HEFCE) has sponsored a project on 'religious literacy', defined as 'knowing what questions to ask, how to ask them, and understanding why they are important'. The goal is as follows:

> By realizing how religion, as a given or chosen identity, is lived in a variety of ways by many thousands of staff and students, we can improve the quality of the learning experience and enrich the daily life of universities and colleges.
>
> (see website)

For some critics there is a 'cake and eat it' quality to these propositions. For others they represent a not so subtle undermining of the mission of the Enlightenment University.

In practical terms it raises the question of how the university organizes its pastoral and personal support for students; as the 'Chaplaincy' becomes something like 'the Office for Student Life' (see Chapter 3). It also puts into a different perspective the discussion (and adjudication) of burning questions that can potentially divide the internal community as much as they do the world outside (for example, 'where do we stand on Israel and Palestine?').

The *ethos* approach does, however, catch a number of recent waves: the hyper-sensitivity about Muslim participation; the anxieties of parents (more than the students themselves) about what first generation participants may be getting into, and the general 'ethical turn' in higher education's response to several extrinsic challenges (as outlined in the next chapter). As discussed in the next chapter, Satan has been replaced by alcohol.

This particular market segment is the best explanation for the development of certain forms of 'outpost' by American and British institutions, sometimes clustered in higher educational 'villages', 'towns', or 'cities', invariably backed by wealthy families and their representatives, and especially in the Middle East. Collectively and individually these initiatives can lead to an intriguing kind of stand-off of competing values. The parents of students from more strictly traditional communities want for their children (notably their daughters) a degree certificate with a global brand, a higher education in English, and insulation from some of the more corrosive dangers of travelling to the West to obtain it. Voices within the 'parent' or sponsoring institutions are more critical of their leaders' willingness, they feel largely for economic reasons, to compromise in particular on commitments to equality around gender and sexuality, as well as dissent in general. A good worked example of these dilemmas is the case of New York University's 'liberal arts and science College' in Abu Dhabi (Lindsey, 2012). Another is the Yale-National University of Singapore (Yale-NUS) College, opening in 2013. Its local president has been forced to admit that students in Singapore will not be allowed to protest on campus or to form political parties (Tharoor, 2012).

Indeed in international terms, it is sometimes hard for the guardians of western university cultures, structured strongly around the Enlightenment values of disinterested inquiry, to understand how comfortable many of their equivalent institutions in other parts of the world can be with living in and seeking to contribute to societies with deep and pervasive religious commitments.

Against this background, it is salutary to reflect on what might be lost in the comfort of the 'ethos' argument. The more severe regimes from which it descended had in some senses higher expectation of university or college membership. Institutional life was (and in some cases still is) structured around not only doctrinal commitment but also practice. Teaching combined (or combines) pastoral and intellectual goals. The chapel was (and is) not a theme park.

Contemporary 'virtues'

A related attempt to keep 'conscience' alive is in the school of thought that sees higher education as fundamentally a source of personal and collective virtue, notably in the work of Jon Nixon (Nixon, 2008), Bruce Macfarlane (Macfarlane, 2004; 2009) and Howard Gardner (Gardner, 2011: see also Watson, 2007: 101–4). Jon Nixon pulls his 'virtuous dispositions' of university life ('truthfulness, respect, authenticity and magnanimity') into a singular 'moral unity' of academic practice (Nixon, 2008: 144,

2). Stephen Rowland goes further by describing 'collegiality' as a form of 'intellectual love' (the term is borrowed from Spinoza). Batting aside his more cynical reviewers, he proposes a 'radical transformation' of contemporary academic culture (which he sees as largely undermined from outside):

> Drawing upon Spinoza's conception of 'intellectual love' I have suggested that if academic enquiry were to be built upon such a unifying conception, collegial relationships would be radically transformed. Trust, openness, collaborative debate and a commitment to knowledge would contrast with the suspicion, self-interest and individualistic competition that are promoted by the marketization of higher education.
>
> (Rowland, 2008: 15)

A 'hard case' arises from another moral panic: cheating. Two drivers in particular have raised the stakes.

The first is the intensification of institutional rivalry about research, not least because of the concentration of supposedly competitive funding (as discussed in the Preface, see also Smith, 2011). The latest spotlight is on medical academics putting their names to articles 'ghost-written' by drugs companies (Fischman, 2012). There are now several watchdog organizations in the USA as well as the Office of Research Integrity (ORI), which has been mirrored in the UK (see website). Boston College's Center for International Higher Education runs an 'HE Corruption Monitor and the Council of Graduate Schools has a 'Project for Scholarly Integrity' (see websites). Devices such as the 'déjà-vu' project and associated software are now in regular use, and there is an emerging consensus that high levels of integrity are linked with high levels of research achievement (Garner, 2009). Universities UK, in collaboration with the funders of research, government departments, and other stakeholders has produced a concordat (with five commitments) on research integrity for all of their supported institutions to sign (UUK, 2012), and the HEFCE is now consulting on whether signing it should be a condition of grant for the institutions it funds (HEFCE, 2012). Other dimensions of academic integrity (or its lack) include relationships with the defence industries, with intelligence services, with recruitment agents, and with governments in general (also discussed in Chapter 5).

The second is the (for some) collapse of student authorship standards in the face of the internet. Plagiarism now has a technical face, and the fear is that the teaching (and assessing) community will always be behind the game. The London *Daily Telegraph* runs a plagiarism league table (see website). For some commentators, application of the US 'honor code' system will make all of the difference here. The model formulation is West Point's 'a cadet will not lie, cheat, steal, or tolerate those who do'. This is the zero tolerance approach to academic malpractice by students that, for example, saw future Senator Edward Kennedy expelled from Harvard in 1951 for having a classmate take a Spanish exam for him (he was quietly reinstated two years later). In 2012 approximately 125 students were made subject to inquiry by Harvard for their collusion in submitting assignments to a survey course in American politics. For others this particular game is shot. Howard Gardner sees the episode as symptomatic of an 'apparent thinning of the ethical muscle of ambitious and privileged young Americans' (Gardner, 2012). The full details of the outcome have not been made public, but we do know that about half of the students involved were required to withdraw from the university for a period, and another quarter placed on academic probation (DeSantis, 2013a).

Even the online course giant Coursera buys in. Students submitting assignments for assessment have to tick a box that states that '[i]n accordance with the Honor Code, I certify that my answers here are my own work, and that I have appropriately acknowledged all external sources (if any) that were used in this work' (J. Young, 2012b). The company is meanwhile exploring whether it can use 'keystroke biometrics' to establish the identities of its students when undertaking assignments (J. Young, 2013a).

We must, however, put student temptations (and their undoubted lapses) into a context where their elders and betters might be said to behave just as badly. In addition to the research communities' temptations (above) there is the delicate interface between graduate (or research) student and supervisor. Here there is not only evidence of bullying, broken promises, dashed expectations, power games, sexual exploitation, and a special form of intergenerational tension, but also a growing casebook of simple theft (Patton, 2012).

What is the enduring legacy of the original drive for securing a good conscience among university students? Can it survive the loss of the anchor of dogmatic discipline?

Chapter 3

The question of character

Over time, this concept of the spiritual purpose of higher education morphed into the notion of individual 'character'.

Behaving well

Moving to a non-doctrinal set of virtues is at the heart of the shift from conscience to character. The fulcrum for achieving this development is, of course, the higher educational philosophy of Newman.

Newman's ideas could be said to be undergoing a worldwide revival, not least in this sense of the existential 'usefulness' of a liberal education. This trend is encapsulated, for example, in some of the discussions of the Harvard 'core' in the United States, of the 'Melbourne model' in Australia (Davis, 2010: 112: Watson 2010: 50–2), and in the UK – sixteen years ago – the Dearing Committee's concerns about breadth as well as depth (Watson, 2007: 141–6). Such a trend could, for example, extend discussion of the 'soft skills' employers say they want into the 'soft citizenship' which is essential to a mature civil society (see chapters 5 and 6 below). It is one important way of ensuring that ethical priorities permeate the life of the academy. One consequence is that the relationship of higher education to the institutions of civil society is increasingly recognized as more important than its role as an instrument of state policy. There is also a powerful international quality to this imperative. Various groups are coalescing around the idea that universities not only have a role securing confident, democratic communities, but also participatory democracy on a global scale (Benson *et al.*, 2007: 111–20; Taylor, 2007).

There are several sources of this revival (independent of Newman's recent beatification).

The first is recognition that life and work in the twenty-first century requires *breadth* as well as *depth* of knowledge and skills. There is, for example, a strong school of thought that 'the skills of a liberal arts major are the best insurance in a rapidly changing world' (this is the conclusion of Jeff Selingo's analysis of the rise in the USA of the 'double-major' phenomenon, especially in 'elite schools' [Selingo, 2012]).

It also revives another Enlightenment idea – delicately probed by Richard Sennett in his sophisticated analysis of 'craft', as what he calls 'the unity of the head and the hand' (Sennett, 2008: 9, 178; see also Chapter 4 below). Think about all of those twenty-first century professions that rely on both cognitive and affective learning. Another manifestation is the rise of what the surgeon Atul Gawande calls 'the science of performance': the challenge of 'implementing our existing know-how' (Gawande,

2007: 232). At the same time the Learned Societies have joined the debate. The British Academy has published a series of reports aimed at establishing the 'public value' of the humanities (British Academy, 2004, 2008, and 2010). The American Academy of Arts and Sciences has followed suit, with a more nationalistic flavour:

> Scientific advances have been critical to the extraordinary achievements of the past century, and we must continue to invest in basic and applied research in the biological and physical sciences. But we also must invest more time, energy, and resources in research and education in the humanities and social sciences. We must recognize that all disciplines are essential for the inventiveness, competitiveness, security, and personal fulfillment of the American public.
>
> (AAAS, 2013: 9)

The second is an 'ethical turn' in public discourse, not least in response to prominent ethical shortcomings in business, professional, and political life. Philip Broughton, in his brilliant account of 'two years inside the cauldron of capitalism', as an MBA student at the Mormon-infused Harvard Business School, describes how Jeffrey Skilling of ENRON went, in the space of this time, from the School's poster-boy to a case study on its ethics course (Broughton, 2008: 19, 44, 157).

The third is a student-led redefinition of mutuality that elevates environmental and international concerns above traditional political allegiances. Look, for example at the revival of student volunteering, at the fact that a majority of UK HEIs now have students from over 100 countries, and that many have a majority of undergraduates who are bilingual.

Finally, and more practically, there is the international growth (as higher education systems become 'universal' with many societies with more than 50 per cent Age Participation Rates [APR]) of second-cycle participation, moving professional formation from undergraduate to postgraduate levels.

We need also to be sensitive to the history of ideas, and the use of words. Newman, for example, coined the term 'the virtual university', by which he meant not some sort of wired-up utopia but the 'habits, manners and opinions' of the world of the 'metropolis' outside (Newman, 1902: 14). What I mean by 'liberal' higher education in its Newmanesque sense is not the same as Newman himself meant by 'liberalism' in the *Apologia pro vita sua* (as 'halfway to atheism' – quoted in Turner, 2002: 9). Rather it is the inculcation of a 'trained faculty', as brilliantly summarized by Owen Chadwick:

> An active energetic force reducing knowledge to order as it is received; a digestion of new evidence into harmony with long acquired evidence; so that this trained faculty can rightly be called an illumination.
>
> (Chadwick, 1983: 53)

Newman (wherever he is) would probably hate it, but I see this as entirely consonant with Sennett's craftsman (see Chapter 4). As the latter writes:

> In the higher stages of skill, there is a constant interplay between tacit knowledge and self-conscious awareness, the tacit knowledge serving as an anchor, the explicit awareness serving as critique and corrective.

(Sennett, 2008: 50)

Nor are these shifts solely western. In February 2012 the *Chronicle of Higher Education* reported on growing Asian interest in the arts at undergraduate level (Fischer, 2012). The result – especially in North America – includes a series of attempts to return the moral educative role of the academy to centre stage.

At a symposium on the life and work of the late Burton Clark, held at the Institute of Education in March 2010, Professor Sir Peter Scott mused on how rich a concept of 'the student' Clark established within his work. Sir Peter went on to reflect that this was not only characteristic of a broader way of thinking about 'student life' within the American system during its most profound period of expansion – connecting the positive value of 'college' with the lives that those who experienced it would lead – but also that Clark maintained this optimistic sense of who students were and what they could achieve right up to the end of a long and very active career, and after several of his distinguished American contemporaries had clearly fallen out of love with mass higher education (and become grumpy old men in the process).

Not a single work by Clark appears in the bibliography of Elizabeth Kiss and Peter Euben's fine collection of essays on the current state of moral higher education, but this sense of the life-enhancing role of undergraduate experience permeates it in a particularly North American way. One of the other points made by Scott was how weak and instrumental our notion of the equivalent 'student experience' has become in British discourse. Duna Sabri makes a similar charge in a recent article on the assumptive world of British higher education policy-makers: 'students are conceptualized either as consumers or as technical learners' (Sabri, 2010: 197).

Kiss and Euben's big question for the colloquium that led to their book is about whether or not universities 'have quit the business of explicit efforts to shape the moral and civic lives of students' (Kiss and Euben, 2010: xi). Their answer, broadly, is that a number of trends point to a revival of interest in exactly such a business. Their 'twelve trends' include new academic interest in 'normative questions', a 're-emphasis on higher education's responsibility to prepare women and men for democratic citizenship', the growth of a curriculum and pedagogy that bridges 'action and reflection' (especially through service learning and community-based research), as well as parallel interests in 'spiritual exploration' and 'practical wisdom'. They also acknowledge that several of these trends make 'many in the academy deeply uneasy' (Ibid. 9–13); a reservation echoed by Patchen Markell's observation that teachers

33

approach these issues with both 'a wariness about moral education' and 'a sense of the inescapability of the ethical' (Ibid. 187).

I use the term 'revival' advisedly. One of the great mysteries of university history is exactly when and how what were essential religious seminaries (in which the college president invariably gave a senior seminar on moral philosophy [Ibid. 249; and Delbanco, 2012: 73] and in some of which a 'conversion experience' was a required part of the curriculum) turned themselves into scientific research machines structured around Enlightenment values. As reflected in the last chapter, Judith Reuben reminds us that 'Harvard was created not just to save souls, but to sustain a righteous community' (Kiss and Euben, 2010: 27). Andrew Delbanco describes a shift in America 'from College to University', associated particularly with the turn 'away from theology' and towards 'the progressive power of science' (Delbanco, 2012: 74–103, quotations pp. 76, 94). Robert Skidelsky, in describing the intellectual environment that formed the young John Maynard Keynes, outlines how Victorian Cambridge lost its faith and found science.

> The 1860s were the decade when Cambridge men lost their religious faith: Edward Carpenter, Leslie Stephen, Henry Sidgwick, Alfred Marshall, Arthur Balfour were all from the 'doubting class' of the 1860s. The decade opened with the consequences of Darwin's *Origin of Species*, published in 1859, and closed with the results of the Second Reform Act of 1867. Occurring more or less simultaneously, the death of God and the birth of mass democracy wonderfully concentrated men's minds on the problems of personal conduct and social order.
>
> (Skidelsky, 2003: 20)

It was only in the previous decade (1854) that Oxford (followed a little later by Cambridge) had, by Act of Parliament, removed the requirement (in place since 1561) that on matriculation (or registration), all students affirmed the 39 articles of the Church of England. It was not until 1871, and the Universities Religious Tests Acts, that the requirement was dropped that fellows of Colleges should be ordained clergymen. In other words, the first 'layer' of university development outlined in Chapter 1 ineluctably influenced the progress of the second.

This is a more complicated story than often appears. Under the influence of liberal education the question of religious conscience took on a less specific concern with character. Meanwhile, as Reuben also points out 'the assumption that science had moral value dominated the discourse about scientific inquiry in the late nineteenth century' (Kiss and Euben, 2010: 35). At the same time professional higher education added its own sets of rules and obligations (although, as David Hoekema notes, these can easily degrade into the primary injunction of 'avoiding civil and criminal liability' [Ibid. 253]). Finally there is the persistent survival (as well as the more recent foundation) of institutions with a strong denominational (if not quite confessional) mission: for example, in the words of Stanley Hauerwas, 'Christians should know what their universities are for' (Ibid. 107). Alongside these powerful vestiges and more generally, many institutions are trying to recapture the social conscience of a former era in a secular age dominated by global communications. As Hoekema also states, for a long time it has been inappropriate to offer 'morality and propriety for a white male Protestant elite' (Ibid. 265). Of course, universities survive in modern society because they transform themselves to meet new needs. Sometimes, however, restoration is as important as change.

Standing in the path of this tide is the eminent Milton scholar Stanley Fish, who in a series of provocatively titled essays in the *Chronicle of Higher Education* (like 'Aim Low', 'Liberalism Doesn't Exist', 'The Same Old Song', and 'Save the World on Your Own Time') puts the counter-case with force and passion. For Fish, given a central role in Kiss and Euben's book (both preceded and followed by critiques of his position), the academic process of 'seeking of truth' is all that counts (Ibid. 88). Here is his golden rule (he admits it is unwieldy):

> In saying or writing this, am I trying to get at the truth about some matter of intellectual concern or am I trying to advance my personal (no doubt deeply held and perhaps useful to society) views about character or about citizenship or about social justice or about anything (remembering always that anything, and certainly these, can legitimately be the topics of an academic discussion as long as that discussion is not politics in disguise)?
>
> (Ibid. 91)

However, for several contributors, like Stanley Hauerwas (Ibid. 99), Fish's residual faith in the value of a 'liberal education' is the Achilles heel in the case of a moral education denier.

In overview, the bulk of the volume shows just how hard it is to reconstruct any kind of moral higher educational consensus. Here are just four of the dilemmas explored:

First, does the traditional focus of institutional attention on the development of the 'whole student' make sense in a context of modern mass higher education? For example, how relevant is what Kiss and Euben call 'the hidden curriculum of campus life' (Ibid. 17) to all of those students who are not young, full-time, and in residence? Is it sensible any more to suggest that the undergraduate years are the crucial stage for the establishment of personal identity, as suggested here by Ruth Grant (Ibid. 287), while modern life-courses in western societies point to young people growing up both faster and more slowly, the latter especially in terms of economic dependence (see Schuller and Watson, 2009: 89–92, as well as Chapter 6 below)? Is this approach inescapably elitist? Elizabeth Spelman talks about the danger of 'distributing moral badges to the already privileged few' (Kiss and Euben, 2010: 121). Should there be a 'conscience clause' allowing those with particular 'private preferences' (the phrase is Alan Wolfe's, quoted in Ibid. 130) to opt out of this form of mandated self-improvement? In other words, are there inevitable tensions between the social and the academic responsibilities of institutions?

Second, is there a way of absorbing multicultural and pluralistic perspectives without giving way to empty relativism? This late twentieth and early twenty-first century challenge to the assumed cultural homogeneity of the early American 'liberal' tradition is probed by several contributors. Notably Lawrence Blum worries about the emergence of 'cultureless' pan-ethnic identities (Ibid. 141) before offering three 'families' of values (pluralism, equality, and community) that should be of resonance in the academy (Ibid. 158). However, is 'acknowledgement' of the other (an obligation originally articulated by Stanley Cavell, and relied upon by several contributors here in addition to Blum) enough? As Wilson Carey McWilliams fears (in a posthumous essay completed by his daughter Susan Jane McWilliams) will 'tolerance' inevitably give way to 'disengagement' (Ibid. 131)?

Third, in the words of Ruth Grant, can we be confident that the humanities will always humanize? 'The same education can make some people better and others worse' (Ibid. 285). To offer a European perspective: the blindness of the German Jewish intelligentsia to the roots of Nazism, painstakingly delineated by Amos Elon and Eric Hobsbawm, may be read as a twentieth-century cautionary tale (Elon, 2002: 355–403; Hobsbawm, 2013: 77–83).

Finally, are there intolerable blind spots in the civic and community roles of HEIs? What about hunger, or poverty? Romand Coles' charge is brutal:

> What does teaching 'values' mean, when many of these values are often articulated in ways that are complicit with this system of power/suffering, or relatively silent about it, or incapable of disturbing the production of deafening indifference or lead only to the occasional trip to the soup kitchen on the way to the oblivious high-paying job in the corporate firm?
>
> (Kiss and Euben, 2010: 224)

Readers from other national systems may dismiss most of this discussion as yet another example of US exceptionalism. This is not least because the book concludes with a powerful dissection of sport within American campus life by Michael Gillespie. What he calls the 'Romanization' (or extreme spectacle) of US inter-collegiate sport is alien to almost every other national system of higher education (Ibid. 311). (Gillespie, incidentally, offers the only extended discussion of gender in the book [Ibid. 314–15]).

However, I think that they would be wrong to do so. The big universal question is whether (and, if so, how) academic integrity and social integrity rely on each other. On this the most telling comments in the volume come from James Murphy, writing about schools, not higher education. He observes the general failure of 'deliberate instruction aimed at inculcating civic virtue', noting simultaneously that (in the tradition of John Dewey) 'academic education is itself a kind of moral education' (Ibid. 171–2). In Newman's final adopted city, the University of Birmingham, supported by the John Templeton Foundation, launched a centre dedicated to the 'character, values and virtues that shape British society in May 2012'. One of its key research questions is 'how does the power of good character transform and shape the future of society?' (University of Birmingham, 2012).

In crude terms the liberal revival does place a premium on teachers knowing (and in some cases restoring) their place. In developed economies they have had to look at two interlinked phemonena: one – rather more long-standing in HE – is alcohol; the second – more episodic – is rioting. Binge-drinking is apparently as prevalent on as off western campuses, and curiously tolerated. Protest is an honourable student tradition, but has become dangerously elided with narcissism (the *Guardian* reports that in its in-depth interviews of 270 participants in the English multi-city riots of August 2011, they established that 'although one fifth … claimed to have no qualifications at all, one in twenty said they had a degree [*Guardian*, 5 December 2011: 7]).

Here is a not untypical cry of pain. Gil Troy, who teaches history at McGill University, reacted as follows to the student participation in a Vancouver riot that followed the loss by the city's professional ice-hockey team, the Vancouver Canucks, of the Stanley Cup:

> It is easier to ignore the problem or blame forces beyond the ivory tower. But college acceptance now offers admission to heavy drinking, drug abuse and risky sexual behaviour. We enjoy a rich intellectual tradition that could trigger valuable debate, favouring moderation and discipline over moral sloppiness and excess without preaching or imposing specific boundaries regarding alcohol, drugs, or sex.
>
> Teaching is not a job; it is a calling. Most of us who became scholars believe in learning's redemptive power. We have a responsibility to help solve the problems plaguing our universities and so we must accept the challenge of stretching our students – intellectually, morally, and psychologically. This fall we should begin a professor-driven moral conversation about binge drinking and the culture of campus partying.
>
> (Troy, 2011)

But apparently 'without preaching or imposing specific boundaries'. Is this another case of having cake and eating it?

In institutional terms the flame kept alive by the American Liberal Arts College is apparently proving worthy of emulation. Another North American example is Quest University (founded as 'Sea to Sky University' in Squamish, British Columbia, Canada in 2002 by David Strangway, a former UBC President). It offers only one degree, and aims 'to prepare young minds to understand and address the deeply complex and rapidly evolving world that they will shortly face' (see website).

Larger, more comprehensive US institutions try to construct such communities somewhat separately within the corporate framework. Examples would be the Harvard College of Arts and Sciences, seen as essential to the 'soul' of the University by its former Dean Harry Lewis (Lewis, 2007), or the fact that Delbanco constructs his compelling defence of the 'College' from within the maelstrom that is Columbia University (Delbanco, 2012). Some of the same thinking may be behind Tsinghua University's move to reconstruct its School of Humanities, dismantled in the post-war 'revolution' between 1949 and 1952, although this initiative may be significantly hampered by censorship and party-political control (Wheeler, 2013). In England, University College London (UCL) has constructed a new BA/BSc degree, following which students will 'learn to be productive global citizens who will be able to make a meaningful contribution to our simultaneously interconnected and fractured world' (Worton, 2013). At the whole institution level the University of Winchester has used these pathfinders as a framework for renewal. In 2010 the University introduced a new programme in the 'liberal arts', designed to foster a 'higher education that embraces ways of thinking that change how we think about ourselves, others and the world in general' (Watson *et al.*, 2011: 180). Its leader, Nigel Tubbs, sees his students as deliberately eschewing the instrumental claims of higher education in a context of economic difficulty:

> As for debts and jobs, students tell us that jobs can wait. If they are going to have to go into debt for their degree, then they are determined to spend their money on something they are really going to enjoy and that does not necessarily mean a degree linked to a career.
>
> (Tubbs, 2012)

Meanwhile, across China as a whole, the number of humanities graduates is growing (from a low base) faster than the scientists. Xing Wei College has been founded as a Liberal Arts institute by a Harvard Business School graduate, Chen Weiming, on the site of a failing technical college. His goal is 'to prepare students for a society that will be different from what they have experienced over the last twenty years'. His initiative thus joins Fudan College (an offshoot of Fudan University since 2005), as well as increased interest by America's liberal arts vanguard (like Williams and Swathmore Colleges) in recruiting directly from China (Ramzy, 2012). Other national outliers of this sort are Campion College in Australia and Lingnan College in Hong Kong (Davis, 2010: 117, 119), while in Chittagong, Bangladesh a number of partners have combined to create the Asian University for Women. This is a residential university, focusing on the liberal arts and sciences, planning to graduate its first class in 2013 (AUW, 2012: 2).

Living and learning together

In practical terms, residential higher education seems to be a critical part of the story. Living together and learning together either does or does not lead to sharing liberal values throughout life and careers. As Harold Silver writes, in an essay on 'abandoning a tradition': 'it is at least surprising that the late nineteenth and twentieth century link between liberal education and residence could so easily be broken' (Silver, 2007: 83–104). Collectively these concerns have motivated a rich literature about something generically called 'campus life'. This encompasses a wide variety of genres: scholarly, promotional, autobiographical, and literary.

The tone of the scholarly genre has been set, in the USA by Helen Lefkowitz Horowitz, and in the UK by Harold and Pamela Silver (Horowitz, 1987; Silver and Silver, 1997). Together they show how religious and communal assumptions have been progressively replaced by both wider and narrower cultural and identity frameworks (the global village and the religious and/or ethnic group), influenced from time to time by politics. If Andrew Marr's *History of Modern Britain* is about the 'defeat of politics by shopping' the story here is about the triumph of the internet over the chapel (Marr, 2007: 97).

In terms of character Horowitz claims to 'have located three distinct ways of being an undergraduate ... college men and women, outsiders and rebels' (Horowitz, 1987: x). 'College life', with its hedonism, construction of elaborate internal institutions (like fraternities, sororities, and societies), and its implicit challenge to the purely educational purposes of the establishment, was born in the late eighteenth and early nineteenth century, against the background of the American Revolution and the early Republic. Opponents were those who never fitted in (sometimes after having tried hard to do so) and rebels are those who were always playing a different game (more 'transcendent', personal, and occasionally political). Writing from within the heart of her own campus (Claremont College) in the mid-1980s, Horovitz is disturbed by its grade-obsessed conformity (or 'grim professionalism' – a term originally coined by Kingman Brewster of Yale to characterize the 1970s) (Ibid. 262, 245).

In the course of the story, the chapel's agent (initially the college president, later the Chaplain [or similar]) has changed. As described in Chapter 2, many American universities now invest in an Office of Religious Life (ORI) and seek to provide a range of denominational and/or counselling officers in support of 'all faiths and none'.

The promotional genre has to do with the market for undergraduate places. This is stronger in richer parts of the world, and those where students traditionally travel to study (and hence to live). In the past quarter-century this market has internationalized – with a vengeance. Claims about the superiority of the 'student experience' at the institution in question are ubiquitous, and rarely grounded in evidence

As for autobiographies, looking back on experience as a student seems to be something people do in writing either very soon after leaving university, or much later in life. Each vantage point can have its blind spots: a lack of perspective, or serious (often nostalgic) memory lapses. Horovitz (above) 'distrusts' them for the purposes of her work (Horovitz, 1987: xiii). The oscillation between evocation of the best and the worst days of a life is omnipresent.

Finally, of course there is the sealed, self-referential genre of the campus story, novel, film, or TV series (in this respect it is a little like the school of the spy story). There have been several analytical attempts at mapping its boundaries, none more successful than Ian Carter's *Ancient Cultures of Conceit* (Carter, 1990). Carter's is a brilliant thought-experiment. Every British post-war university novel trapped in a van fused in a tunnel in Wales following a nuclear Holocaust. From this material the agents of a superior civilization eventually reconstruct the twentieth-century British university (Ibid. 4). Needless to say, this is nearly all about Oxbridge; and the Colleges more than the Universities (Ibid. 38). Students hardly feature, until very recently. Meanwhile various sorts of 'otherness' are all deprecated: 'proletarians, scientists, women and foreigners' (Ibid. 69). He also concedes that in terms of imagination and bite American campus novelists (Nabokov, Wolfe, Malamud, McCarthy, Barth, Lurie) write their 'English competitors off the page' (honourable exceptions are C.P. Snow and David Lodge) (Ibid. 211).

The features of living together, playing together and (occasionally studying) together make this a rich tapestry for transformation claims (see also Chapter 7). From time to time there are moral panics, about security, about sports (especially in America), about political interference (or too much political passion), about in- and out-group tensions (leading to speech and behaviour codes, and the critics of their apparent political correctness), about shared decision-making (especially the role of students in university governance), about 'town vs. gown', and even about the priorities set between campus rules and the civil and criminal law (with special concerns about double-jeopardy). One such wave of concern led the Carnegie Foundation (led by Ernest Boyer) to investigate campus solidarity in the late 1980s. Their *Report* recommended six pillars upon which the campus could reconstruct its sense of communal identity and purpose: the college or university community should seek to be educationally purposeful, open, just, disciplined, caring and celebratory; perhaps also thereby offering 'a model for the nation' (Carnegie Foundation, 1990: 7–8).

The moment might have passed, other than in those institutions which specifically seek to preserve or re-create the liberal concern for character, or what Boyer calls the colonial-seminarian 'concern for the whole person' (Ibid. 5). The modern college or university finds it understandably hard to be a perfect microcosm of the wider world.

Today the question of the university as a physical location has a different set of resonances to 'dormitory' life. A lot of contemporary pedagogy depends on what could be called 'short distance learning'. Today's members of the university (staff as well as students) are permanently connected to the network, even if they are sitting just outside the library or the classroom (they can also be 'connected' inside – in the latter case with contentious results). This has led James Lang to promote the concept of the 'grounded campus' and 'grounded curriculum': 'a radical re-imagining of the campus and the town as a laboratory for more and more experiments in teaching and learning' (Lang, 2012). In many ways this is an 'inside-out' reciprocal of the 'civic engagement' narrative that had a central place in so many institutions' founding documents (Watson, 2010).

It has also come under pressure from the full range of distance, part-time, and 'blended' types of pedagogy, as well as from its costs. This is Peter Lampl, founder of the UK Sutton Trust (an advocacy organization for widening participation) on the arrival of the MOOCs (see Chapter 1):

> I learned as much if not more from my fellow students than I did from the lectures ... But they're the things – making life-long friends, joining a society, learning how to operate a washing-machine – that are free. It's the education bit that's the expensive part. But what Udacity and the rest are showing is that it doesn't necessarily have to be.
>
> (quoted in Cadwalladr, 2012)

Being 'useful'

'Character' moves the 'conscience' argument on in some interesting ways, not all of which would have been congenial to Newman. Jane and Leland Stanford said that their university (named on its opening in 1891 in memory of their son Lee, who had died of typhoid in 1884) would 'qualify its students for personal success and direct usefulness in life' (see website). In particular the focus shifts to 'service' and 'usefulness' or, in other words, to how the beneficiaries of higher education elect to behave.

It is appropriate to return at this stage to Newman, although I want to offer a quotation demonstrating an aspect that is often underplayed when assessing his basic stance (it is from Discourse Seven, on knowledge and professional skill):

> If then the intellect is so excellent a portion of us, and its cultivation so excellent, it is not only beautiful, perfect, admirable, and noble in itself, but in a true and high sense it must be useful to the possessor and to all around him; not useful in any low, mechanical, mercantile sense, but as

diffusing good, or a blessing or a gift, or power, or a treasure, first to the owner, then through him to the world. I say then, if a liberal education be good, it must necessarily be useful too.

(Birnbaum, 2004: 124; see also Furlong, 2013: 169)

Much of this chapter, of course, presupposes that we can determine what 'character' is, as well as what measures we can apply to its increase or decrease in individual cases. One way in is to look at the ways in which scholarships and other forms of personal investment or reward are assigned when qualities other than academic performance (or 'merit') are in play. A survey by Carrie Hauser of the Ewing Marion Kauffman Institute of non-cognitive attributes as they are used by American scholarship organizations for minority candidates reveals use of the following (among other devices): the emotional intelligence (EQ) index; 'resilience' (as shown when, for example, 'reframing adversity' as a positive challenge); scores for 'self-concept' and 'social engagement'; as well as the ability to construct a narrative of key events in the candidate's life (Hoover, 2013). Many of these would also be relevant to curriculum and pedagogy once inside higher education, especially in contexts where the creation and reinforcement of positive character traits is an objective.

Has the concept of the College Man (or Woman) survived the modernization of the academy? Combining behaving well with being useful opens up a wide spectrum from honour codes to volunteering in the community. It does, however, move us on from conscience to character. Today – except in those institutions for which this is the raison d'être – there is less opening of the window into men's (or women's) souls. In terms of popular culture, character is robust and enduring. To end this digression with Tallulah Bankhead:

I read Shakespeare and the Bible and I can shoot dice. That's what I call a liberal education.

(Birnbaum, 2004: 126)

Chapter 4

The questions of calling, craft, and competence

This leads on to various more traditional theories about 'useful' higher education, including the deep vein termed 'vocational'.

The 'professional formation university'

The professions were there from the beginning, and have influenced the story throughout. Universities have always had an intimate relationship with the 'professions', not only producing 'professionals' but also creating and subjecting to rigorous critique the content of professional knowledge. In the later Middle Ages the relevant cast of disciplinary characters included lawyers and theologians, as well as (often forgotten) rhetoricians and musicians.

In the early modern period public servants of various kinds ('administrators') were added to the mix. A classic Tudor example would be the mathematical pioneer Robert Recorde (1510–58). Born into an established family in the port town of Tenby (his father was mayor in 1519), he was sent to Oxford at the age of 15 and at 21 was elected a Fellow of All Souls. In 1535 he moved to Cambridge, where in 1545 he graduated in medicine. There followed a remarkable series of publications: in mathematics, *The Grounde of Artes* (1543); in medicine, *The Urinal of Physick* (1547); in geometry, *The Pathway to Knowledge* (1551) and *The Castle of Knowledge* (1556); and in algebra, *The Whetstone of Witte* (1557). In the latter he is attributed with having introduced the 'equals' sign (=) to modern mathematics. Alongside this early-modern academic contribution there was, however, a full-blown professional career, principally as a Controller of Mints (in Bristol, London, and Ireland) and surveying mines (in Ireland). At the same time, Recorde had to try (and ultimately failed) to manage the religious swirl of public life (including, as a strong supporter of Henry VIII's break from Rome, the Marian reaction). He died in prison (Baldwin, 2010).

By the seventeenth century, across Europe, the professional focus was fully re-orientated – to serve the emerging state. Rosemary O'Day has demonstrated this set of developments in England:

> To say that the universities lost control of the professions is too simple and far from accurate. They maintained a firm grasp on preparation for careers in the church and the civil law. New professions grew up outside the universities' formal control. However, the new professions were influenced by the universities in many ways, some formal and some

informal. Leadership of the new professions often rested in university-educated men who revered learning. The ethos of the gentleman (which had developed at least in part in the universities) spread to the professions.

(O'Day, 2009: 99)

Philip Withington goes further in terms of celebrating the democraticizing and 'useful' power of higher education expansion:

Political consciousness was heightened by the expansion in educational provision during the 16th century, based on a curriculum that brought classical learning, including Greek and Roman philosophy into the vernacular. By 1640, on the eve of the civil war the proportion of eligible men in further education was higher than at any time before the mid-20th century.

(Withington, 2012)

Moving on, in the great age of higher education foundations of the late nineteenth and early twentieth centuries, science and technology (broadly understood – to include, for example, architecture) had their day in the sun. The professional institutions and societies (many based in Britain) had their heyday spreading a model of professional formation through higher education around the world. Indeed if you tour their headquarters in London you can get a feel for where they came from and where many of them have ended up. The classic example is the home of the Institute of Civil Engineers, at 1 Great George Street: still a cathedral of global reach (its main hall is constructed of varieties of stone from across the world) and now an upmarket conference centre.

In the late twentieth century the various professions of the service and creative economies joined in. In this phase many complex occupations previously characterized as 'craft' (for example art and design) achieved appropriate recognition of their role within the higher education enterprise. Law and medicine (latterly health in general) have been there throughout, as have educators of various kinds since the nineteenth century. The early twenty-first century has followed the postmodernist spirit of the times by adding to the professional palette new domains such as capital markets, niche journalism, alternative therapies, and events and hospitality management (Cunningham, 2008).

In his highly original account of how the field of 'education' was absorbed into the academy, and with what implications, John Furlong quotes Jaroslav Pelikan on the curiously liminal position that professions can take up: of and between both the worlds of professional practice and of scholarship: 'The university protects them from becoming the vassals of the profession; the profession, in turn protects them from becoming mere satellites of the graduate school of arts and sciences' (Pelikan, *The Idea of the University* [1992] quoted in Furlong, 2013: 3). As Furlong's careful analysis reveals, however, this is not how it has always felt. As a forty-year veteran of the public sector of UK HE, as well as undertaking a stint at the University of London's Institute of Education, I read his narrative feeling a little like the drowning man going down for the third time. Furlong's thesis is that 'education', inextricably entwined as it has been with 'teacher education', was kept at arm's lengths by the mainstream, even when authoritative reports (like Robbins in 1963) urged its integration, and when it finally did make it (largely as a result of the changes in status of the former public sector polytechnics and large colleges, in 1988, 1992, and 2004) it was too late:

> The end of the twentieth century not only saw the final arrival of education as a university-based discipline, but … also the fundamental restructuring of the university system. As higher education and science became increasingly important instruments of national economic policy, it was more and more difficult to think of academics as self-regulating communities.
>
> (Ibid. 26, 110, 146)

This is referred to several times as a pyrrhic victory. His solution is, however, not far away from that suggested below in Chapter 8, in 'practical wisdom' (Aristotle's *phronesis*) and the Enlightenment project of the 'maximization of reason' (Ibid. 9, 176, 178, 180).

A popular contemporary fad relates to entrepreneurialism. According to Howard Stevenson of the Harvard Business School, '[e]ntrepreneurship is the pursuit of opportunity without regard to the resources currently controlled'. This has sometimes been translated as doing what you want to do for which you don't yet have the means.

The 'entrepreneurial university' has become a familiar trope in recent discourse, reflecting the instrumentalist drive for higher education to appear useful, as well as to stimulate and enhance economic growth. As several observers have pointed out, Burton Clark's book on *Creating Entrepreneurial Universities* sits on the bookshelf behind almost any vice-chancellor giving a TV interview (Clark, 1998). Meanwhile there have been attempts to soften the concept, in particular by embracing 'social entrepreneurialism' (see, for example, the work of the Skoll Foundation, as set out on its website).

Oxford's Saïd Business School runs a course for entrepreneurial university leaders, and there has been a clutch of books ranging from the empirical (Shattock, 2008) to the exhortatory (Thorp and Goldstein, 2010). The 'entrepreneurial university' is one of the eight models that take the higher education theorist Ron Barnett from the 'metaphysical' to his preferred 'ecological' university (the others are 'scientific', 'bureaucratic', 'liquid', 'therapeutic', and 'authentic' [Barnett, 2011: 33–44]). Above all, there is a drive to teach 'entrepreneurship', paradoxically in the same set of breaths as teaching 'employability'.

Returning to the professions more specifically, upgrading to higher education contexts, and graduate status has not always been easy, given the understandable defensiveness of established professions and from time to time the unrealistic expectations of those promoting or investing in the change. Nursing and several of the professions allied to medicine would be a case in point. In the UK it has been a long haul from the emergence of the first initial (as opposed to post-registration) degrees in the 1980s to the confident conclusion of the Willis Commission in 2012:

> The commission found no major shortcomings in nursing education that could be held directly responsible for poor practice or the perceived decline in standards of care. Nor did it find any evidence that degree-level registration was damaging to patient care. On the contrary, graduate nurses have played and will continue to play a key role in driving up standards and preparing a nursing workforce fit for the future.
>
> (Willis Commission, 2012)

It is important to acknowledge the role of student choice in creating this palette. They have generally led the market, while the providers have been stuck in the mode of wishful thinking exemplified by the recent waves of STEM initiatives. The result can be a particular institutional form, which I call the 'professional formation university'. The University of Brighton is an example. It has developed essentially as a confederation of professional schools, created at different times by a community perceiving different needs. The timeline of the foundations of its constituent parts is as follows. The two key gathering points were obviously the Polytechnic in 1970 and the University itself in 1992.

- 1859 The School of Art
- 1897 The Municipal School of Science and Technology
- 1898 The Chelsea School (evacuated to Borth in 1939, moved to Eastbourne in 1949)
- 1909 Brighton Municipal Training College
- 1947 Brighton School of Librarianship
- 1963 Brighton College of Technology
- 1965 Brighton College of Education
- 1970 Brighton Polytechnic
- 1979 Merger with East Sussex College of Higher Education
- 1990 School of Physiotherapy
- 1992 University of Brighton
- 1994 Institute of Nursing and Midwifery
- 2003 Brighton and Sussex Medical School
- 2004 University Centre Hastings
- 2013 University Centre Central Sussex (Crawley)

What does the future hold for the 'professional formation university'? On the face of things 'professions' and the now ubiquitous 'skills plus employability' agenda should go hand in glove. However, in my view the 'professional formation university' faces some particular challenges. These are not just about professional accountability, discipline, or that toxic phrase of Adam Smith's, 'a conspiracy against the public'.

As indicated above, universities have always had an intimate relationship with the 'professions', not only producing 'professionals' but also creating and subjecting to rigorous critique the content of professional knowledge. Meanwhile, over the last half-century the public service professions have moved steadily towards, and frequently into the university. Both teacher education, and more recently health professions have bet on our being able to do a better job than they were able to do outside. However, as the drive to cut back on public sector expenditure intensifies, it may lead to the economic difficulty of 'guilt by association', whereby public servants are seen (often unfairly) as unduly protected.

At the same time, one consequence of the revival of 'liberal' higher education (outlined in the last chapter) may be the global movement of professional formation from undergraduate to postgraduate levels. Another is that we shall have to challenge the Professional and Statutory Bodies (PSB)-led 'crowded curriculum' of many British professional courses, in which the content requirements of licensing bodies squeeze out wider educational objectives and opportunities.

As set out in the Preface (above), what counts in league tables (like research citations and self-evaluation by members of academic fields) is the opposite of most of the features that governments say they want from 'their' institutions (like high teaching quality, contributions to social justice and entrepreneurialism), even when they simultaneously set targets for, say, top-100 finishers. Professional formation sits uneasily in this narrowly competitive world. Some elite forms count – like law, medicine, and executive business education. The vast majority do not.

The 'professional formation university' may also have to deal with institutional hybridity in a rather special way. It should be at the forefront rather than in the slipstream of the messier, more fluid system of higher education that today's society requires. The big picture is that as a system the UK is going to have to become less precious, more flexible, and significantly more cooperative (this links with the discussion in Chapter 6 of lifelong learning). To take a worked example, we are going have to be more like one half of the North American system.

Politicians and commentators who look at the USA generally fixate on one or other of two models: Harvard or the California Master-plan. Incidentally, each of these is in trouble at present, for differing economic reasons (Rothblatt, 2012; Bidwell, 2013). This polarity contains a fundamental principle, concealed by the 'national average' data put out by the Organisation for Economic Cooperation and Development (OECD) and others. Slightly fewer than half of American undergraduate students go to four-year public or private residential colleges and universities, and a respectable number complete their degrees on time. Meanwhile the rest have a much messier route. They often complete their Bachelor's degrees in institutions other than the ones in which they started, with gaps, a mixture of full- and part-time study, a lot of experience of earning while learning, and above all by accumulating credit for what they achieve along the way (Weko, 2004). According to the National Student Clearing House Research Center's report on *Transfer and Mobility* (NSCH, 2012) one-third of all students change institutions at some time before earning a degree, a rate that is consistent across all types of institutions outside the for-profit sector (where the rate is lower). Slightly more part-time students transferred than full-time students. Of those who transfer: 37 per cent transfer in their second year; 22 per cent transfer as late as their fourth or fifth year; 25 per cent transfer more than once; 27 per cent transfer across state lines; and 43 per cent transfer into a public two-year college (NSCH, 2012: 5). Meanwhile, even the prestigious institutions are ready to accept each other's course credit, to admit students with advanced standing, and essentially to play the CATS (credit accumulation and transfer) game (Azevedo, 2012). Because of the success of this messier system, about 60 per cent of the population has a serious experience of tertiary study, and in popular culture 'college' is positively referenced and valued.

The UK system has to learn to emulate this. Instead in policy, funding and public perceptions of HE, it looks to lock in all of the features of the wrong half. For obvious reasons this poses challenges to received wisdom about professional formation.

Among the steps needed to realize this goal is to return to the development of Credit Accumulation and Transfer (CATS). In *Learning Through Life* (discussed further in Chapter 6) the Commission on Lifelong Learning argued that the flexibility which a proper credit framework brings will be needed all the more in the light of current economic turbulence and the effects this is having on employment. Large numbers of adults will be seeking to improve their qualifications without having to commit themselves to a long stretch of full-time education. Our conclusion was stark: 'This is not a technical issue: we have the systems. It is a cultural and moral issue: we fail to use these systems for reasons of conservatism, snobbery and lack of imagination' (Schuller and Watson, 2009: 145–55).

At several stages both the sector and the government have made CATS a high policy priority. For example, at the time of the *Dearing Report* in 1998 New Labour declared in their Green Paper, *The Learning Age*, that they wished to see a fully functioning credit transfer system by 2000 (DfEE, 1998: para. 6.18). There have also been endless efforts to calibrate and promote such systems. An example, including the hype of its launch in 1999, was SCOTCAT (Scottish Credit Accumulation and Transfer – see SCQF, 2003: 2). Across the sector as a whole the outcomes have been feeble, although the OU remains an honourable exception (Di Paolo and Pegg, 2012). There are both regional and national groups trying to keep the flame alive, like the South East England Credit Consortium (SEEC) (see its website), and the UK Credit Forum (UKCF) (see Bridges and Flynn, 2010). However, most of their impact has been within further education (FE) or at the FE/HE border. Formally, at least the UK is also a participant (via some complex convolutions over comparability) in the European Credit Transfer System (ECTIS) (Sweeney, 2013: 12).

It was not always so. The formation of the Council for National Academic Awards (CNAA), the foundation of the Polytechnics and the expansion of Public Sector Higher Education (PSHE) in the 1970s and 1980s brought about a major drive for flexibility in course design and assessment as well as mode of study (Watson, 1989; Allen and Layer, 1995). A major report by David Robertson, *Choosing to Change*, arrived probably at exactly the wrong time, as institutions from across the former binary line sought to position themselves in the aftermath of the 1992 Further and Higher Education Act (Robertson, 1994). Further confusion was caused by devolution (for example, the Dearing Committee struggled to align the Scottish HE qualification framework with that of the rest of the UK [Watson and Amoah, 2007: 13–14]).

Pressures militating against the success of CATS in UK HE have been varied. Most important has been institutional protectionism, reflected especially in the reluctance to grant advanced standing. This is reinforced by a funding approach that devalues part-time and mixed-mode study. Then there is cultural rigidity; a British lifelong learning journey is nearly always set in stone by the first step taken (e.g. the theory of the 'royal route'). Within universities an unempirical and poorly theorized pedagogy based on 'meritocracy' (that believes, for example, that getting something right first time – rather than after some effort – means that it has been more securely learned) takes its toll as does comparatively slow progress on assessment of prior and especially experiential learning (APL and APEL). This has led to the victory in many institutional settings of 'subject' over broader, including interdisciplinary and multidisciplinary interests. Finally these are compounded by a 'management' error (made interesting by both of the significant modular pioneers – now Oxford Brookes and London Metropolitan Universities) that having many subject combinations on offer is inherently inefficient.

It is worth thinking hard about how to revive and more securely embed the opportunities for learners, their sponsors and institutions, which could be brought about by a more generous and less risk-averse approach to credit. Properly approached, it will be shown to link with: pedagogical innovation (including reflective learning and the recording of achievement); individual life-chances (notably 'learning and earning'); career and community development; and strategic institutional responsiveness (to research, development, and service needs, as well as to the student market).

In the face of challenges like these, the professional formation university will have to keep its nerve. Its goal is to produce graduates who have not only knowledge and skills, but also wisdom and judgement. Above all this will require a focus on what

Howard Gardner and his collaborators call 'Goodwork': professional work which is 'of excellent technical quality, ethically pursued and socially responsible, engaging, enjoyable and feels good' (Gardner, 2007: 5). Whether or not this remains a socially desirable and validated role will depend on the next phase in the long march of the professional formation university.

The 'craft' revival

Meanwhile, we have another revival in progress, of interest in the higher reaches of 'craft'. In his *The Culture of the New Capitalism*, Richard Sennett sets out the concept of craftsmanship, as one of his three potential sources of a 'social anchor' in what is otherwise a rather pessimistic view of the prospects for twenty-first century work and personal identity (the other two are 'narrative' and 'usefulness'). For him 'craftsmanship' is 'doing something well for its own sake'. It is linked with democracy, via the 'citizen-as craftsman', and it is structured around 'commitment'.

> It's not simply that the obsessed, competitive craftsman may be committed to doing something well, but more that he or she believes in its objective value. A person can use the words correct or right in describing how well something is done only if he or she believes in an objective standard outside his or her own desires, indeed outside the sphere of rewards from others. Getting something right, even though it may get you nothing, is the spirit of true craftsmanship.
>
> (Sennett, 2006: 104, 171, 195)

This is a very powerful metaphor for what is going on in higher education. It is, I believe, a 'craft' in the sophisticated sense that Sennett describes. It is also about more than just the alliance of the head and the hand. As he says in *Together*, 'I cannot believe that social experience is disconnected from physical sensation' (Sennett, 2012a: 219).

It is no accident that in Britain the origins of non-university tertiary education were very substantially constructed around the notion of 'craft'; in 1850 there were over 600 'Mechanics' Institutes' serving over 100,000 students (Sims, 2010: 20–3). This powerful stream of market-responsive higher education had its characteristic pedagogy, and was regarded as profoundly liberating by many of its participants. Its nemesis was, however, the traditional university world, and its progressive colonization (through its own examination boards) of the system of public examination, shifting it from a confirmation of capability to a competitive entry gate.

Once again there has been a twentieth-century flattening out of these priorities, as caught by the modish preference for 'skills', competence, and (the only just literate) 'competency' and their (only just logical) plurals, 'competences' and 'competencies'.

'Higher skills'

'Higher skills' are a special piece of code. In the UK they have been an important part of government ideology – on the part of all major parties – for at least the past quarter century. The Conservatives began, with their National Education and Training Targets from the mid-nineties (Cassels, 1990). New Labour followed on with the *Leitch Report* of 2006 (Leitch, 2006), and the same view of human capital animates much of the rhetoric of the post-2010 Coalition Government. However, the ideology covers a number of fracture points, to do with: 'general' or 'transferable' vs. 'specific' or 'occupational' skills; 'supply' and 'demand' sides of the market; and deep ambivalence on the part of employers who say they want one thing (e.g. relevantly qualified graduates) and act differently (for example, in screening for the social prestige of providing institutions). The notion of 'competence' is itself deeply problematic (Barnett, 1994).

The result includes some deep ambivalences, for example about what is often negatively termed 'credentialism', 'commodification', or 'instrumentality'. There is a fear that young people are being under-sold a higher education experience by short-term, and often tactical approaches to qualification for a job market that is itself in a serious state of flux (I return to discuss the concept of employability in Chapter 6). At this point two correctives to this basically ideologically loaded critique are in order. First, students themselves can often be more aware of the dangers of narrow and constricting career opportunities, which many of the 'skills' advocates are unashamedly promoting, than many of their elders and betters (Alison Wolf evocatively invoked the apparent oxymoron of the 'rational teenager' to describe this phenomenon [Wolf, 2002: 88]). Secondly, it can underestimate the inherent renewal and refreshment values of the best of the craft and professional traditions of education. Rob Fraser and Andrew Thompson combine the two ideas in their description of the 'new artisan'. This person 'embodies the cross-disciplinary skills and entrepreneurial aspirations that are pivotal to economic growth, and specifically to wealth creation opportunities from the digital economy'. More specifically she or he will 'bring craft, design, science, art and ingenuity to the task' (there are shades here of the 'media studies' boom of the 1990s). Their example is from Microsoft (Fraser's employer), which directly employs 3,000 people in the UK but also has 260,000 qualified persons working with its technology, not just in STEM-related fields but also all across the service and creative economies (Fraser and Thompson, 2012).

There is also a link here with what employers recruiting from the international market say that they want. Here is a list of graduate attributes favoured by a survey from the Council of Industry and Higher Education (CIHE) in 2008:

- Communication skills   82% (86% non-international)
- Team-working skills   91% (88%)

- Integrity   85% (76%)
- Intellectual ability   79% (67%)
- Confidence   64% (81%)
- Character/personality   73% (88%)
- Planning/organization skills   70% (86%)
- Literacy (writing skills)   67% (60%)
- Numeracy   73% (62%)
- Analysis/decision-making skill   76% (71%)
  (Source: CIHE, 2008).

Both the validity and the utility of exercises like this are questionable. They are dip-stick tests of what employers think rather than what they do. For example, the acid test is whether they search intensively enough for institutions and courses that take such requirements seriously, or are content merely to screen by institutional reputation.

Are all skills subject to a market test? Is having a vocation an essential part of living in and contributing to contemporary society?

Chapter 5

The question of citizenship

What exactly are the obligations of the university and its members to civil society, to the state, and to wider international interests?

The university in civil society

All would agree that the university occupies a critical role within civil society. There is a corollary: when it becomes over-identified with the political interests of the state, it has probably lost its way. The *Urtext* of this error is Martin Heidegger's Rectoral Address to the University of Freiburg in 1933:

> Out of the resoluteness of the German students to stand their ground while German destiny is in its most extreme distress comes a will to the essence of the university. This will is a true will, provided that German students, through the new Student Law, place themselves under the law of their essence and thereby first define this essence. [Proclaimed on 1 May 1933, the *neue Studentenrecht* sought to organize students according to the *Führerprinzip* in an effort to integrate the universities into the National Socialist state.]
>
> To give oneself the law is the highest freedom. The much-lauded 'academic freedom' will be expelled from the German university; for this freedom was not genuine because it was only negative. It primarily meant lack of concern, arbitrariness of intentions and inclinations, lack of restraint in what was done and left undone. The concept of the freedom of the German student is now brought back to its truth. In future, the bond and service of German students will unfold from this truth.
>
> The first bond binds to the national community [*Volksgemeinschaft*]. It obligates to help carry the burden of and to participate actively in the struggles, strivings, and skills of all the estates and members of the people. From now on, this bond will be fixed and rooted in the existence of the student by means of *Labour Service* [*Arbeitsdienst*].
>
> The *second* bond binds to the honour and the destiny of the nation in the midst of all the other peoples. It demands the readiness, secured by knowledge and skill and tightened by discipline, to give the utmost in action. In future, this bond will encompass and penetrate the entire existence of the student as *Military Service* [*Wehrdienst*].
>
> The *third* bond of the students binds them to the spiritual mission of the German people. This people works at its fate by opening its history to

all the overwhelming world-shaping powers of human existence and by continually fighting for its spiritual world anew.

(see website)

As David Phillips has demonstrated in a number of searching studies of post-war educational reconstruction in Germany, putting this sort of thinking right was a daunting task, and has its resonances in all sorts of post-crisis/post-conflict situations (think of Afghanistan, Iraq, Libya). He quotes Field Marshal Montgomery in his role as the first Military Governor of the Occupation Forces addressing the 'Population of the British Zone' in August 1945:

> 10. The reputation of your Universities fell low in the world's esteem under the Nazis. Their buildings suffered severe damage during the war. I shall allow no professor or lecturer to continue in office who prostituted his gifts in the service of the Nazis. Buildings will be restored where possible. ...
>
> 15. You German fathers and mothers must do your part to win back your children to a saner way of life. I shall help you. You must help me. That is my order.
>
> (Phillips, 2012: 573)

The sticking point is well articulated by Michael Daxner, former Rector of Oldenburg University and post-war EU Education Commissioner in Kosovo. 'East of Vienna', he has said, 'the role of universities is in society-making, not state-making'. Universities are needed, he says 'because of our dangerous knowledge' (quoted in Watson, 2007: 41). The notion of 'dangerous knowledge' – that is of being critical as well as supportive of activities across civil society leads to moral injunctions for both states and their universities. To illustrate that this is more than just a theoretical issue, consider the current struggle in Iran for control of the Islamic Azad University (Yong, 2010), or in Egypt for the soul of Al-Azhar, founded in 970–2, and arguably today 'the most celebrated educational institution in the Muslim world'. In 2013 it is described as 'being stalked by every player in the country's nascent democracy' (Vick and Khalil, 2013: 28).

We may also have got it wrong in the UK in terms of 'citizenship education'. A brittle, nationalistic, quite possibly politically colonized view of what it is to understand and project rights and responsibilities as a member of a democratic and inclusive society is unpersuasive to many of that society's members (particularly youth and minorities of various kinds) and has been allowed to disguise a much more generous, contemporary sense of what it is to be a citizen. The scholarly literature points to several dangers: a perennial 'deficit' model (especially where young people are concerned); a rhetorical trend that moves very quickly and uncritically from rights to duties; a presumption that obedience and patriotism are inviolable; and a consequent ceding of the case for change to extreme groups of both the right and the left. As Jürgen Habermas puts the problem, '[t]he fusing of citizenship and national culture results in a 'monochrome' interpretation of civil rights that is insensitive to cultural differences' (Habermas, 2005: 3). It can also be ideologically captured. In September 2012 central Hong Kong was brought to a standstill by protests against 'national education lessons', to be made compulsory in primary schools by 2015 and secondary by 2016 (Liu, 2012).

Universities are central, for example, to a former Prime Minister's conception of 'Britishness':

> The qualities of British life – the notion of civic duty binding people to one another and the sense of fair play which underpins the idea of a proper social order – come together in the ethic of public service [giving rise to] the great British public institutions admired throughout the world ... [among them] our universities, including the Open University.
>
> (Brown, 2004)

The *summum* of this point of view is probably the 'Life in the UK' test, now mandatory for British citizenship and settlement, and memorably described by Sir Roy Strong (on GMTV on 21 January 2009) as a 'quick romp around New Labour Britain'. An updated version in 2013 could be said to move the politics on (a little like those much despised textbooks from authoritarian regimes, or George Orwell's 'Newspeak'). The textbook for this version talks about Margaret Thatcher and the decline of traditional industries with no reference to the miners' strike except for the impact of 'too powerful unions ... harming the UK' (Booth, 2013; see also website). The test itself continues to require boning up on a highly specific history of immigration, as well details from the census, knowledge of a long string of 'national' and religious dates (like 'Mother's Day'), knowledge about quangos, political processes (like 'what are the roles of whips?'), constitutional matters such as the Act of Succession, the composition and role of the European Union (EU), Commonwealth and United Nations (UN), and finally knowledge on how to behave on the motorway, in estate agents, post offices and pubs (Watson, 2009: 35–9). Speaking at the Hay Festival in May 2010 the author (and Chancellor of the University of Durham) Bill Bryson said that he had not become a British citizen because he feared that he would fail the test. David Cameron, Brown's successor as Prime Minister would sympathize. On 27 September 2012 he was ambushed by the American talk show host David Letterman with a series of citizenship-style questions. Cameron guessed that 'Rule Britannia' was composed by Edward Elgar (not Thomas Arne) and failed to translate the term *Magna Carta* (he did, however, retrieve the date of 1215). 'Boy, it would be good if you get this right', murmured Letterman (Watt, 2012).

What politicians, and some university leaders, are looking for here is a type of 'common preparation' for what they regard as acceptable civic life. Bruce Smith and his fellow authors outlined this for the United States in a celebrated book, called

Closed Minds? For them the goal of 'a shared educational experience, a common liberal education, and preparation in the broadest sense for citizenship in our democratic society' had receded (Smith *et al.*, 2008: 14). Democracies, in particular, can find this hard to deliver.

In other national contexts, identity politics can become toxic, and leak into the university, as in ethnic preferences on selection. In some, higher education will become almost a part of national service, with a military flavour. In others, aspects of history, language, literature, and other disciplines with strong elements of partial heritage will loom uncomfortably large.

Every national system is, of course, different. Hence the importance of the American 'law school' question – what's the jurisdiction? The legislative and administrative framework in any country will normally affect at least three things: governance (strategic direction, appointment of leaders, accountability); funding (direct and indirect controls, e.g. fees); and operational conditions (subjects and levels of provision, conditions of employment, procurement etc.).

This is where the felt effect of the layering of foundations (as set out in Chapter 1) comes in. The issue is not so much the diversity of institutional types (also discussed in Chapter 4) as colleges and universities each try to find their way towards the sunlight of economic and reputation success. For this there are many celebrated classifications, of which the US-based Carnegie system is the most frequently utilized (see website). More influential is the jurisdictional framework provided by legislation and public funding (or its lack). This has led to distinctive systems emerging in: North America (a mixture of public and private institutions, with relatively relaxed approaches to institutional title and accreditation); Britain and its former Empire (with a strong presumption of official funding co-existing, sometimes paradoxically [see the Preface], with higher levels of institutional autonomy); Continental Europe (with largely state-sponsored institutions given freedoms, including at faculty and departmental levels, which governments are now trying to roll back, including through the transnational initiatives on qualification levels set since 1999 by the Bologna process [Sweeney, 2013: 10]); and finally a Nordic model, in which the presumption of public interest (and funding) is probably the most advanced. Newer state systems are apparently free to cherry-pick from these broad models, constrained though they are by demands for growth in student numbers and the precarious state of public finances.

At present some very interesting dividing lines are opening up in higher education between (broadly) the global North and West, and the South and East.

On the one hand you have the values, attitudes and priorities of North America, Britain, Ireland, continental Europe, and Australasia (and in certain respects Scandinavia). In the North, universities derive much of their moral power from simply 'being there'; they are aware of their influence as large players in civil society. They will stress their role in developing character and democratic instincts (see

Chapter 3). They will focus on contributions like service learning and volunteering (see below). Their model of economic contribution is 'knowledge transfer'. And they will see public support – for these and other roles – as an entitlement.

Meanwhile across much of Asia, Africa, the sub-continent, and Latin America, things look different. As the authorial team established in *The Engaged University* (Watson *et al.*, 2011), looking from the South to the North, exposes the lack of any such comfort zone. For one thing it can simply be more dangerous in the South; violence can be around and in some cases on the campus itself.

University campuses in the global North and West can have their own problems with violence. Sometimes this is about location, and it is an interesting test to see how easy or difficult it is for non-members to gain physical access, including for the most innocent of reasons (perhaps to enjoy the 'green lung' of a university site in an area of relative urban decay). Certainly once border security is tightened up it is almost impossible to go in the other direction and relax it. The Ivy League contrasts the fortress that is Yale in New Haven with the sprawl of the University of Pennsylvania throughout the ravaged western end of Philadelphia (in response to a crime wave in 1996, President Judith Rodin turned several of the buildings around so that they opened out into the community rather than back into sealed quadrangles [Rodin, 2007: 59–80]). Some British universities face the same dilemmas, sometimes highly successfully (like Queen Mary, University of London [QMUL] in East London).

With disturbing regularity there are then gun-related episodes on American University campuses (as there have been in schools) with the related discipline of lock-down drills. The massacre at Virginia Tech in April 2007 in which 33 people died represents a link in a disturbing chain of regular such events (Hauser and O'Connor, 2007). James Fox (who monitors these events) points to an average of 20 mass shootings a year in the US over the past three decades, each resulting in at least four deaths (Fox, 2012; Fox and Burstein, 2010).

This is not quite the same as being a university in a conflicted or post-conflicted society. Many universities in the global South and East have found ways of managing to stay open, and productive, in extremely harsh and unforgiving environments. A graphic recent case – which did lead to closure – was the armed incursion in October 2012 into the Federal Polytechnic in Mubi, Northern Nigeria. This resulted in 46 student deaths by shooting: the pretext was a student union election (Mark, 2012). In January 2013 the Syrian civil war swept through the University of Aleppo, leaving many dead (O'Malley, 2013).

Also in the South and East there is frequently a central political drive for outcomes like 'transformation' (South Africa) or 'solidarity' (Latin America) (Leibowitz, 2013: xv, 47). There is a privileging of 'development' (or social returns) over 'character' (or individual returns); and of 'national cohesion' over personal enrichment. There is a strong focus on human capital, and 'employment' over 'employability'. 'Necessity trumps choice', and investment in HE is seen as more than a consumer good. There will regularly be greater use of private bodies for public purposes, and of international partnerships for assistance rather than 'positioning', as well as fewer hang-ups about the instrumentality of the 'vocational curriculum'. There is also an acceptance that religion and science should work in harmony (see Chapter 2), and in many cases, a profound understanding of the kind of 'trade' that Habermas sees as vital in not just a post-Enlightenment, but also a postmodern world:

> The understanding of tolerance in the liberally constituted pluralistic society asks not only that the believer have the understanding that she has to *reasonably* reckon with the persistence of disagreement in dealing with believers of other faiths. The same understanding is asked of the non-believer in dealing with the believer. For the secular consciousness this implies the non-trivial requirement to *self-critically* determine the relation between faith and knowledge from the perspective of worldly knowledge.
>
> (Habermas, 2005: 27)

In terms of the economy, there is evidence of a very practical world of 'Mode 2' engagement, alongside Mode 2 research and teaching. Above all 'being there' doesn't cut much ice; there is a much greater sense of societal pull over institutional push (Watson, *et al.*, 2011: 240–9; see also Leibowitz, 2013).

'Soft' citizenship

James Arvanitakis and Bob Hodge, in the very practical context of working with both high school and university students in Greater Western Sydney, have neatly encapsulated the 'top-down/bottom-up' dilemma of defining citizenship:

> The figure of the citizen and the surrounding practices and discourses are ambiguous and incorporate a double gaze. From above, it is a strategy of governance and a way to incorporate segments of the populace into an alignment with ruling sections of the state. From below, it is a strategy for relative empowerment. The balance here varies: rather than a pre-fixed concept of the citizen, citizenship is a site for struggle that is constantly redefined in the process.
>
> (Arvanitakis and Hodge, 2012: 61)

I am working on an alternative conception to the brittle, nationalistic version of citizenship, termed 'soft citizenship', and I suggest that universities are its natural seed-bed (see also Arthur, 2005). The potential link to other forms of currently approved 'softness' (like 'soft skills', 'soft power' – and even 'female' characteristics of leadership) is deliberate. So too is the echo of Timothy Garton Ash's 'liberality', including 'generosity, open-mindedness and freedom from prejudice'. This is the final of his 'pentagram' of liberal values, designed to help 'defend and enhance the freedoms of an open society in conditions of growing diversity'; the others are 'inclusion', 'clarity', 'consistency', and 'firmness' (Garton Ash, 2012).

The stress here will be on not just self-awareness, but also awareness of others, and of deeper senses of sympathy and connection than civic conformity will ever bring about. In so far as institutions succeed in stimulating and nurturing it, they contribute to the more individual sense of personal responsibility and capacity for 'public reasoning' outlined in the final chapter of this book.

The currently fashionable concept of 'academic citizenship' plays a role here, as does Howard Gardner's exposition of the educational enterprise as a type of 'commons' (Macfarlane, 2007; Gardner 2012). Academic communities at their best stress ways of behaving, intimately connected with the scholarly enterprise (see the 'oath' in Chapter 7) that provide serious models of practice for the real world. More experienced learners (see the 'conversation' in Chapter 6) can act as role models for the less experienced. They can also, at their best, supply safe environments in which conflicts (of ideas, of distribution of goods, or of political, social, and economic entitlement) can be tested out.

In summary, the rounded – or 'soft' – citizen will have various valuable attributes: a sense of loyalty; a balance of scepticism and trust; a commitment to progressive engagement with wicked or intractable problems; and a presumption that knowledge can inform responsible action. All of these have been, and can continue to be nurtured by the university.

The international campus

At the heart of many of these issues is the new condition of the international campus. All around the world, university campuses have reverted to a position that they often occupied in their initial European phase of development: of being more cosmopolitan than the societies that surround them. Now with transport by aircraft and an intense international market for student recruitment, a majority of British universities have students from more than 100 countries (Watson, 2007: 33). At the same time, traditional routes for student mobility have diversified radically. It is peculiarly satisfying in Oxford to see the portrait of the founder of the Rhodes scholarships and his contemporaries in the Masonic austerity of Rhodes House gaze down on the rainbow nations of today's scholars.

Cosmopolitanism thus enters the picture. And as Kwame Anthony Appiah concludes in his *Cosmopolitanism*, the kind of 'conversation' that structures higher education at its best vital to value adjudication, especially in circumstances where 'there are some values that are, and should be universal, just as there are lots of values that are, and must be local' (Appiah, 2006: xxi). However, the prospects and benefits of global awareness can be both under and over-sold. The 'international experience' offered by those countries most aggressively marketing undergraduate, and especially short-cycle and lucrative postgraduate courses, can seem hollow when the students who have travelled long distances find themselves in 'enclaves' of their countrymen and women, using their native language together, tactically managing the curriculum and assessment from this base, and above all failing to connect with either the rest of the university, or even their host society. This can be especially problematic in non-English speaking environments (see Morita, 2012). It is important to note that this is not a culturally imperialistic point; 'English' has become not only the language of the internet, but also the language of tradable international higher education, as well as a magnet for third parties to study in countries such as Germany and Sweden. Even France, and especially the Académie Française, is getting nervous, as the government seeks to relax a law (dated 1994) that requires all instruction to be in French (De La Baume, 2013).

A combination of worldwide recession, heightened security concerns (sometimes coupled with xenophobia, and even racism) and ICT has led to a paradoxical return of one aspect of nineteenth-century global HE. A over-heated, air-travel-based market in higher education has been replaced by a new pattern of cooperation in the provision of HE (admittedly for shared economic interests) between first world, emerging market, and developing countries). MOOCs are relevant here, as is the probable end of the bubble of establishing branch campuses (like the University of Nottingham's Ningbo, China, established in 2004 – which remains an outlier, rather than a pioneer: see website). Australian institutions, in particular, have discovered the costs of 'teaching out' courses in overseas colleges that never met their ambitious initial projections (for a cautionary tale, see the story of the University of New South Wales – motto 'Never Stand Still' – in Singapore [O'Keefe, 2007]). At the same time it is salutary to acknowledge that the magnet effect of traditional national leaders is matched by their own conservatism in exporting students: during the rapid expansion of this international trade the big 'importers' slowed down in their rates of sending their own students elsewhere (de Wit *et al.*, 2013: 19).

Nor is this the only source of tension. Universities can find it hard to meet the requirements of different groups as they seek to maintain safe arenas for the discussion of hard questions; gender segregation at meetings is a current example (Ibraheem, 2013). Governments can find it hard to square the circle of income generation and domestic security. Especially since 9/11, the clampdown via visas and other border controls, designed to keep the community safe at one level (but at another often playing into nativist and intolerant hands), have had a particular impact on higher education. The principal cases are the United States, which found its supply of postgraduate students in science and technology almost terminally squeezed, and the UK where the temporary revocation of the UK Border Agency (UKBA) licence to recruit students from outside the EU of London Metropolitan University sent shockwaves throughout the system (Morgan, 2012c).

Brain drain and brain exchange then enter the picture, with complex issues about students wanting to use HE qualifications to escape their origins, about pressure on labour markets in a time of recession, and the potential flight of professionally qualified people from poorer countries. Such economic pressures have all but drowned out an older notion of higher education opportunity as an arm of public diplomacy, with established systems taking pride in the education of future leaders around the world.

However, every so often HE cosmopolitanism gains an eloquent and compelling advocate. One such was Aung San Suu Kyi, receiving her honorary degree from Oxford in June 2012:

> Oxford taught me to value humankind, because when I was in Oxford I was the only student from Burma. I think I was the only Burmese person resident in the university for the first couple of years. And all my friends were non-Burmese – of course English students, but students from all over the world, from Ghana, from India, from Thailand, from Sri Lanka, from all over the world. And I never felt that they were different from me. We were all the same: we were all students of this university, which has some magic that makes us feel that nothing separates us – neither religion, nor race, nor nationality, nor even different levels of excellence in academic affairs. Oxford is a place of tremendous broad-mindedness. Nobody discriminates against anybody else because he or she may be different, or may not have achieved as much as others. Every human being is expected to have a value and a dignity of her kind or his kind. And that's why throughout the years when I was struggling for human rights in Burma I felt I was doing something of which my old university would have approved. And to feel the approval behind me has helped me a great deal.
>
> (see website)

The student estate

All of this has modified the concept of the student estate. In the heightened atmosphere of 1968, Eric Ashby and Mary Anderson attempted to map the legitimacy and the limits of the concerns of the 'student estate':

> It is concern which unites the more sensitive members of the student estate to the rest of their generation. They will not break this tie. Practical evidence of their concern for society is of course something for students to work out for themselves; they must not expect paternalism on this any more than on other issues … But the students who display this social concern still need to be assured that the scholarly virtues of objective study and intellectual detachment can coexist with concern for humanity. They

> fear that detachment really means indifference and objectivity means impersonality. If this fear is not dispelled mistrust and cynicism may spread into an epidemic of anti-intellectualism. It is an essential task of university teachers to dispel this fear.
>
> (Ashby and Anderson: 1970, 155)

One of the key related issues for this study is the condition, including in political terms, of the student estate. Culturally there has been an almost universal assumption about student radicalism: students are meant to be idealistic and to want to change the world, and this has been expressed in different ways in different places and in different times. More recently this has been supplanted by a discourse – said to be more in tune with mass participation and economic stringency – of instrumentalism and 'employability' (as also discussed in the next chapter).

But, as usual, the story is more fine-grained and complex than it first appears. What may appear as indifference to traditional (especially partisan) politics, may simply reflect transference of energy and attention to other issues and other ways of wanting to change things. Several analytical zones are separable.

The first is the extent to which student-based groups are an independent or quasi-independent force. It is very clear, for example, currently in Chile and Thailand that the major political parties and movements have to take account of what students and their leaders think and want.

The second is the impact of student protest, about their own condition or that of others. Many societies in the North and West have been genuinely surprised about the scale and intensity (including violence) of protests against higher fees and other aspects of cuts in public support for HE. In Quebec the anti-fees alliance *Classe* brought down the provincial government. In Germany, students were at the heart of the movement that caused the *Länder* to back off on fees (Mechan-Schmidt, 2013). Earlier examples (in 2009 and 2010) were California, Austria, and the United Kingdom (Friend, 2010; Morgan, 2009; Vasager *et al.*, 2010).

Third, it is useful to establish the position of the university as a source of state support, opposition or even, in extreme cases, of refuge. The latter arises most starkly in the case of Greece, where the controversy over the repeal of Law 1268 (which has forbidden the entry of police on to University grounds since 1982) rages on (Mavrogordatos, 2012).

Finally there is the transnational force of students as campaigners on specific themes such as the environment or social justice. Nowadays any significant 'alternative' or protest gathering does not take long before it establishes its own 'university'.

This process links with at least two honourable traditions: the 'free' university, and heroic autodidactism. In each there is a strong seam of Paolo Freire's 'pedagogy of the oppressed' (see Freire, 1998). Thus the 'tent-city' universities of the post-credit-crunch 'Occupy' movement (see website) link back to the Free University of Berlin (founded in 1948 as a protest against the Soviet-dominated Humboldt University, and at the head of worldwide student protests in 1968) and forward to the Free University of Liverpool in 2011 (Cloughton, 2011). And thus, many of the registrations on MOOCs from poorer parts of the world, as well as the theory of Anya Kamenetz' *DIY-U* (Kamenetz, 2010), and Dale Stephens' UnCollege (see website; also Fazackerley, 2013) go back to Hardy's Jude Fawley (Watson, 2008c). A calmer, and more established, example is the UK's University of the Third Age (U3A), with, at the time of writing, nearly 900 centres and nearly 300,000 learners (see website).

As implied by the concept of the student estate, the university also acts as a corporate personality, reconciling (to the extent that this is possible) the various interests that make it up: students; staff of various kinds; and genuine external stakeholders. This in turn raises the question of responsible institutional behaviour. Universities can behave well, or badly. In 2008 I listed some of the ways in which universities (most of the cases here were from the USA) could fail to live up to their ethical corporate ambitions. They included: athletics, hazing, merit vs. need in financial aid, endowments, and independence (including 'legacy' admissions); brokering private funding, studying abroad, league tables, free speech and academic freedom, independence in research, and grade inflation (Watson, 2008b). Steven Cahn has worked for years on cataloguing similar moral problems in American higher education (Cahn, 2011: viii-ix). Writing today, not least in the aftermath of the meltdown of the nation's most successful college football operation (Penn State, in the wake of the conviction of assistant coach Jerry Sandusky for sexual abuse of minors in his charge), it is easy to feel that things have simply got worse (Freeh *et al.*, 2012).

A number of slippery-slope issues come into play here. Minor misdemeanours, failures of judgement, and especially their cover-up can escalate into a corporate culture of bad behaviour. Student groups are among those first to seize on the double-standards of zero tolerance for students (see the discussion of honour codes in Chapter 2) and apparently infinite tolerance for employees (especially academic staff). Some double standards are very odd indeed. Eric Schwitzgebel earned himself an award for the discovery that academic ethicists are the group most likely to steal books from their university libraries (Schwitzgebel, 2009).

Internal corruption can be matched (or exceeded) by corrupt influences from outside. They can all too easily collude with unethical practice, for example through the use of recruitment agents (on payment by results) in the international recruitment market (Bergman, 2012). Institutions can find it hard to maintain their ethical compass in the face of pressures relating to funding (public and private), participation (not only who gets in as a student but also who gets the jobs), prestige (association with the regime – as notably in the case of Heidegger – or just the 'right people' – including dominant ethnic and/or economic groups), and politics.

The vexed question of who pays even enters the fundraising arena as the desire for respectability on behalf of potentially compromised individuals and groups meets the appetites of institutions for funding streams and endowment independent of the accountability framework of the public purse.

When there is money on the table – or even the whiff of money around the corner – institutions can lose their ability to make sound collective judgement. An example is the treatment by the London School of Economics (LSE) of the doctoral candidacy of Saif al-Islam Gaddafi, son of the deposed Libyan leader, currently held by the new Libyan regime. Several elements came together here: domestic political pressure, the history of the LSE and its leaders in advising an overseas regime, the prospect (and the delivery) of lucrative contracts, the use by a high-profile student of external consultants in the preparation of a thesis, and concerns about the standards set in a doctoral examination. All of these were painstakingly unravelled in an inquiry led by former Lord Justice Woolf reporting in October 2011. Among other things, he reveals how one institution was able to make a clear decision on the candidate's eligibility as a research student (Oxford determined that the 'bottom line' was that he was not qualified), and another simply passed the problem around internally because no one authoritative was prepared to accept the consequences of such a judgement (Woolf, 2011: 28). The Director of the LSE, himself directly implicated in some of the decisions, had resigned before the report was published.

Perhaps here a strange kind of statute of limitations is also in play. As the Cambridge classicist Mary Beard puts it in her popular blog:

> I certainly suspect that many of the founders of Cambridge Colleges acquired their cash in decidedly dubious ways, but we have been doing good with their ill-gotten gains for centuries. In a way that counts as a moral transformation.
>
> (Beard, 2012: 172)

Students, their institutions, and their supra-institutional networks and organizations, thus sit within a number of concentric circles, including that of political power. Their influence varies, but is permanently latent.

Chapter 6

The questions of conversation and capability

What are the roles of higher education in inculcating 'life-skills', including employability?

Conversations old and 'new'

Nothing set out so far is intended to undermine the traditional essence of higher education (what is genuinely 'higher' about it) in terms of the evolving 'conversation' between more and less experienced learners. Indeed the higher education enterprise could be said to be a model of the form of conversation, the loss of which is lamented by Stephen Miller in his elegiac *Conversation: a history of a declining art* (Miller, 2006). This insight was endorsed by the Dearing Committee in its rather lengthy chapter on learning and teaching (NCIHE, 1997: 114–29). Miller draws extensively on another theme of Michael Oakeshott's: for him conversation is 'an unrehearsed intellectual adventure'; as with gambling 'its significance lies neither in winning or losing, but in wagering' (Miller, 2006).

Theodore Zeldin concludes his *Conversation* (based on a series of talks given on BBC Radio Four) as follows:

> What is missing from the world is a sense of direction, because we are overwhelmed by the conflicts which surround us, as though we are marching through a jungle which never ends. I should like some of us to start conversations to dispel that darkness, using them to create equality, to give ourselves courage, to open ourselves to strangers, and most practically to remake our working world, so that we are no longer isolated by our jargon or our professional boredom … That is what I call the New Conversation.
>
> (Zeldin, 1998: 97)

Capability and lifelong learning

Such conversations should lead to 'capability', as in the work of Amartya Sen. For Sen, 'capabilities constitute the capacity to achieve well-being'. In his *The Idea of Justice* he explains further:

> Freedom to choose gives us the opportunity to decide what we should do, but with that opportunity comes the responsibility for what we do – to the extent that they are chosen actions. Since a capability is the power to

do something, the accountability that emanates from that ability – that power – is a part of the capability perspective, and this can make room for demands of duty –what can be broadly called deontological concerns.

(Sen, 2009: 18–19)

Richard Sennett, in his treatise on cooperation (*Together*) draws on Martha Nussbaum to link capability and the critique of inequality: 'she remarked that a capability sets a standard not just for what human beings can do but also for how society may fail to nourish them' (Sennett, 2012a: 147). Turning to higher education, Melanie Walker has been the principal advocate of Sen's capability approach as the basis for constructing and refining curriculum and pedagogy. In her hands it is seen as bringing together 'engaged learning, agency, and change' as well as (in the spirit of Sarah Mann's analysis of the roots of alienation in the undergraduate experience) 'a deep ethical concern with the development of each and every student as an end in themselves [sic]' (Walker, 2006: 17; Mann, 2001).

In the report of the Inquiry into the Future for Lifelong Learning (IFLL), *Learning Through Life*, Tom Schuller and I identified key areas in which a responsible and comprehensive system of learning should inculcate capabilities, such as the digital environment, health, finance, and civic life (Schuller and Watson, 2009: 223).

This is where higher and 'continuing' education meet. The report went back to first principles. We were very conscious that 'learning' is a complex and often paradoxical proposition, of which higher education is only a significant part. Some learning takes place in institutional settings: in schools of all levels and types; in colleges and universities; in places of worship; as well as in clubs and societies. A lot of it does not; for example, the *workplace* is both a significant site for learning, and a platform for learning elsewhere. Sometimes learning has to be collective; sometimes it is profoundly individual. One of the *mantras* in compulsory education at the moment is around 'personalization' (framing the educational experience so that it is just right and just in time for the individual learner). Of course this can work well, but there is a danger in suppressing the shared understanding that comes from learning together. Some learning requires formal recognition (as in accreditation) before it is of value; other learning will remain not only personal but also private. Often learning is joyful; sometimes it requires pain, and especially endurance. You sometimes have to frighten yourself into learning what it is you have to learn. Above all learning is about an attitude of mind, a propensity, or a curiosity. It isn't just about subject knowledge; nor is it just about practical skills. It is also about developing the judgement needed to put these two together. Many people refer to this as 'learning how to learn'. There is a final paradox: some learning is instrumental or routine; other learning is liberating or transformative. We learn to earn, but we also learn to live. The report's vision was of 'a society in which learning plays its full role in personal growth, prosperity, solidarity and local and global responsibility' (Ibid. 8–9).

Consequently, as a group the Commission began from the premise that the right to learn is a human right, connected with these aspects of the over-arching vision. Our instincts were against compulsion and fixed formulae. Above all we did not want learning to be used as a weapon to impose uniformity, or a narrow view of individual, social, or economic development. In so far as *Learning Through Life* sets out a framework, it is a framework of opportunity, structured around investment, incentives, and capabilities. Our goal was to set an agenda for lifelong learning that would make sense for the next quarter-century. Overall, we were struck by how much of the current dialogue and interventions in learning are dominated by analysis of deficit and its remediation. A consequential priority was to move much of the language of the debate beyond dismissal and condescension. A related goal was to assist our society in moving past fixing things (often with unintended consequences) to realizing the genuine personal, social, and economic benefits of lifelong learning. The ambiguity in the title – *Learning Through Life* was deliberate: we believe in both learning through life experience and throughout the life-course.

In summary, *Learning Through Life* asserts that access to learning throughout life enriches and strengthens individuals and societies. To secure this right, it makes proposals on ten major fronts.

The first was to base lifelong learning policy on a new model of the educational life course, with four key stages (up to 25, 25–50, 50–75, 75+). Our approach to lifelong learning should deal far more positively with two major trends: an ageing society and changing patterns of paid and unpaid activity.

It is helpful to look at these revised stages in turn. Our first perception is that the transition through and beyond compulsory education and into young adulthood is taking longer. There used to be an assumption that that this occurred around 16, then 18; now it's not until around 25 that directions appear to be set. In the UK in 2006, 58 per cent of men and 39 per cent of women aged 20–4 were living with their parents. Young people are growing up both faster and more slowly; cultural independence is juxtaposed with economic dependence. Then there is the heartland experience of work, family and other responsibility, and (it seems) temporarily declining satisfaction (these are the 'time pressure' years). Next, the assumption that this continues until we simply fall into official 'retirement') at 60 or 65 seems to be receding. We found evidence of an increased *negotiation* of types of work and responsibility from the mid-50s onwards. And why should the next quadrant (50–75) be the end? We drew on the substantial evidence that learning in older age (75–100) can reduce dependency as well as enrich life.

In response, the report proposed rebalancing resources fairly and sensibly across the different life stages. Public and private resources invested in lifelong learning amounted in 2009 to over £55 billion (about 3.9 per cent of GDP – and going up to something like £93 billion if we add in opportunity costs); their distribution should reflect a coherent view of our changing economic and social context. At present, the allocation of resources for learning is approximately as follows across the four quarters of a potential one hundred year life-span: 86: 11: 2.5: 0.5. The report proposed that it should be modestly redistributed by 2020, as follows: 80: 15: 4: 1. What is more, the adjustment costs of this change would be reduced by the increasing fit with the demographic realities of an ageing society.

Thirdly, it proposed building a set of learning entitlements. Structurally, we felt that some entitlements should be universal, including basic skills at all ages and a 'threshold' or 'platform' to step off into lifelong learning, from the equivalent of high school graduation and university matriculation, as well as access to IT. Above all lifelong learning should foster not a crude selective meritocracy (as in Michael Young's satire, discussed below) but recurrent opportunity. Others should relate to working life. 'Learning Leave' is a powerful device here, possibly to be funded by redeploying the £3.7b of corporation tax relief now granted for training. Yet others could support voluntary and involuntary transitions (such as a 'welcome' entitlement for those crossing borders to join new (for them) communities, or leaving institutions such as prisons or care.

At the same time there is a need to engineer flexibility, via a system of credit and by encouraging part-timers. Much faster progress is needed in the UK to implement a credit-based system, making learning more flexible and accessible with funding matched to it. Crudely, and as set out in Chapter 4, we have the systems, but we are very reluctant to use them. The Commissioners felt that adopting approaches to funding that are agnostic as to mode, across the whole array of post-compulsory education is vital to unlock this potential.

Above all, there is a need to use learning to improve the quality of work. The debate on skills has been too dominated by an emphasis on increasing the volume of skills. There should be a stronger focus on how skills are actually used. As stated in the report, there is currently 'a naïve belief that upgrading qualifications for the population as a whole will produce all of the benefits which are only accrued by the subset of people who currently have those qualifications' (Ibid. 31). Going back to the life stages, it is necessary to understand what is happening not just in the middle, but across all three of the latter stages. Our suggestion is that economic activity should be recognized up to 75 (and not 60–65 as at present). We need more of elements such as accreditation, and notably of what have been identified by Lorna Unwin and others as 'expansive' rather than 'restricted' learning environments at work (Unwin *et al.*, 2008). There is an equity issue here too. Access to training diminishes down the status ladder.

As suggested above, in terms of content, the report proposed constructing a curriculum framework for citizens' capabilities. A common framework should be created of learning opportunities, which should be available in any given area, giving people control over their own lives. There should be a common core of provision: of content (initially around digital, health, financial, and civic capabilities – the downsides of lacking these are all too clear), of local and contextual customization, of quality assurance, and of support for teachers and other key 'intermediaries' (examples are Citizens' Advice Bureaux advisers, probation officers, and health visitors).

This led on to recommendations about broadening and strengthening the capacity of the lifelong learning workforce. Stronger support should be available for all those involved in delivering education and training (including intermediaries like these).

The next two points flowed together. First, there was a drive to revive local responsibility. The current system in England has become over-centralized, and insufficiently linked to local and regional needs. We should restore life and power to local levels.

This could be achieved by a variety of steps: stronger local strategy-making, by local authorities; greater autonomy for Further Education (FE) colleges, as the institutional backbone of local lifelong learning; stronger local employer networks; a major role for cultural institutions; and local Learning Exchanges: for connecting up teachers and learners, providing a single information point, social learning spaces, and an entitlement 'bank'.

Secondly, national frameworks matter. There should be effective machinery for creating a coherent lifelong learning strategy across the UK, and within the UK's four nations. We need to have a single department with lead authority, and another body to check on progress.

And finally, it was suggested that we have to make the system intelligent. The system will only flourish with consistent information and evaluation, and open debate about the implications. In this context the Commissioners proposed a triennial 'State of Learning' report. The first such report is unlikely to be very encouraging. Consciousness of demographic pressures is growing, and has sparked some creative (as well as some panicky) thinking about pensions, and the need to reduce the retirement cliff-edge. Massive health service reforms could both support and undermine the necessary preventative public health agenda. Entitlements to learning support continue to fluctuate wildly, including according to political fashion. New school models (free schools and academies) threaten to undermine the 'full service' school project. Devolution (and the prospect of a Scottish Independence vote) could continue the process of Balkanization of policy, provision, and performance.

From the higher education perspective the UK (led by England) is increasingly an outlier in the disappearance of its ambition to expand rather than control and contract the availability of places. However, it maintains its position as one of the most lifelong learning-friendly systems in Europe, with, for example, a strong record in admitting mature students: 31 per cent of first-time undergraduates are aged over 21 on entry, and 14 per cent over 30 (McVitty and Morris, 2012: 7–8). Meanwhile the overall pattern of participation in higher education has almost defeated the politicians' almost exclusive emphasis on the young, full-time undergraduate student. More than half of current registrations are now on other modes and levels of study, with the fastest rate of growth at the second cycle.

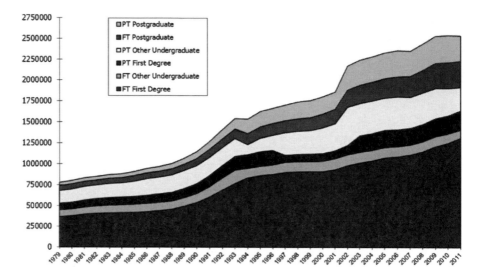

Figure 6.1: Number of HE students by mode of study and level of course, UK, 1979–2011

Source: DES 1991–2; DfE 1994; HESA 1996–2013

'Graduateness' and 'employability'

From the policy perspective, a vital issue here is what is intended by the concept of 'graduation'. What capabilities do graduates bring to their experience of employment? This section draws on a long experience of often circular discussions about 'graduateness'. What are 'graduate attributes'?

At the height of the UK 'quality wars' the Higher Education Quality Council (HEQC) thought that it would nail this question once and for all in its 'Graduate Standards Programme' (GSP). Unfortunately this initiative, like a lot of such taxonomies collapsed in the end under its own weight (Watson, 2006). The trick seems to be to marry institutional and programme specificity with wider educational goals. Thus the University of Melbourne has linked its new undergraduate curriculum model (discussed in Chapter 3) with a list of 'attributes of the Melbourne graduate' under the headings of 'academically excellent', 'knowledgeable across disciplines', 'leaders in communities', 'attuned to cultural diversity', and 'active global citizens' (Watson *et al.*, 2011: 51). Thus too, Queensland's James Cook University attempts to cement its goal of creating 'a brighter future for life in the tropics worldwide' by creating graduates who are:

committed to lifelong learning, intellectual development, and to the display of exemplary personal, professional and ethical standards. They have a sense of their place in the tropics and are charged with professional, community, and environmental responsibility. Quite central to their commitment is their need to embrace and be acquainted with Australia's First Nations Peoples and Singapore's First Nations Peoples, reconciliation, diversity and sustainability. They exhibit a willingness to lead and to contribute to the intellectual, cultural, and social challenges of regional, national, and international communities in the tropics.

(see website)

A similar list (like JCU's carefully constructed to address local circumstances) is at the heart of Stellenbosch University's 'pedagogy of hope for the post-apartheid Republic of South Africa' (RSA). A graduate of this institution is a person who (in an attractive mixture of the present and future tenses):

- is well rounded and whose potential has been enhanced to the fullest;
- is competent and equipped for professional life;
- is adaptable and equipped for lifelong learning;
- can play a leadership role in society as a responsible and critical citizen in a democratic social order;
- is capable and equipped through the application of their [sic] high-level skills, to play a constructive role in the responsible and sustainable development of the country and society, and who, in so doing, contributes to the well-being and quality of life of all people;
- is equipped to function effectively in a multilingual context.

(Leibowitz, 2013: 90)

A related question to 'what are graduate attributes' is what is a 'graduate job'? The temptation is to answer, 'whatever a graduate gains', or 'whatever job a graduate does'.

Here are some headlines I collected from newspapers in the summer of 2011, as the recession began to bite in the United Kingdom (this is the point at which the Futuretrack generation, discussed below, graduated). They all raise the question 'Is HE worth it?' They point to:

- The decline in the 'graduate job market' ('Record 83 graduates chase every job vacancy', *The Sun*, 28 July 2011).
- Average graduate debt of £60,000 ('Students face leaving university with £60k debts', *Daily Telegraph*, 23 August 2011).
- 200,000 qualified students unable to get into university in September 2011 ('Four students competing for each university place', *The Guardian*, 22 August 2011).

- The falling away of the much vaunted 'graduate premium' ('So is it worth getting a degree? One in five graduates is earning less than a school leaver', *Daily Mail*, 25 August 2011).
- Employers' groups, which six months ago were saying that a degree was essential to professional progress, now saying that it isn't ('Degrees? Get straight to business instead', *Daily Mail*, 21 August 2011).

In these circumstances the question – is HE worth it? – can be seen as provocative. It is a question that is put with even more force than usual following a period of great expansion and in a time of economic recession. I have also noted that it is a question that is usually put by people who have been to universities about those who have not (yet). I remember an episode of the BBC TV programme *Question Time* when the perennial question of whether we need more graduates or plumbers was raised. After four of the panel had frothed at the mouth about the 'mindless expansion' of higher education, the fifth, the actor Tony Robinson looked tellingly along the line and said 'I notice that everybody who says that fewer people should go to university went to university themselves; I didn't, and I rather wish I had'. We are in a strong era of 'pulling up the ladder'.

There is a powerful literary rehearsal of some of these arguments in Zadie Smith's comedy of manners of the ethnically mixed contemporary North London estate, *NW*. The heart of the story is the relationship between two children of the estate, one black (Keisha, then Natalie Blake) who becomes a high-flying lawyer, one white (Leah Hanwell) who marries an African immigrant and takes up what she regards as a dead-end job in a community arts organization. The trajectory of the story takes them away from the neighbourhood to university, and then back, if to radically differing circumstances. Their mildly dysfunctional families, of course, never leave. Smith does not belabour the point, but it is very clear that in many ways each discovers who she is at university (Smith, Z., 2012).

There are also other dynamics at play. Leah's (black) boss Adina is proud of having 'the graduate' in the office, while it occurs to her that 'no one – not the institution that conferred it, not her peers, not the job market itself – has a higher estimation of the value of her degree than Adina'. This is not how Leah herself looks back:

> What was the point of it all? Three years of useless study. Out of pocket, out of her depth. It was only philosophy in the first place because she was scared of dying and thought it might help and because she could not add or remember lists of facts or speak a language other than her own. In the university prospectus, an italic script over a picture of the Firth of Forth [the University was Edinburgh]: *philosophy is learning how to die*. Philosophy is listening to warbling posh boys, it is being more bored than you have ever been in your life, more bored than you thought it possible to be.
>
> (Ibid. 28–9)

The question – 'is HE worth it?' – collapses a lot of other questions concerning for whom it might be 'worth it'. I'm going to offer four angles on this difficult topic.

Theorists often reduce this to a discussion of *capital*. What kind of capital does higher education set out to create? I have addressed this question in Chapter 1.

Secondly, this type of analysis moves on to questions of *motivation*. This mixes rational with affective (or emotional) assessments. The issue of 'rates of return' on investment in higher education (of money, time and emotional energy) is very complex

It is one of the fundamental premises of this book that universities are membership organizations and that the co-creation of knowledge involves almost everybody working in them. In my experience most students grasp this proposition with comfort and integrity; they know they cannot simply purchase a degree. This does not, of course, prevent them from being appropriately demanding about facilities, (the 'hygiene' factors) about support, and about the accuracy and completeness of the information they are given about how they will be taught, assessed, and communicated with.

In the UK (and in some similar jurisdictions) government has built on this latter set of considerations to find another way of holding institutions to account. At the undergraduate level the government has a touching faith in the power of informing the purchaser. Here is David Willetts, the minister for universities and science, writing on the day that the 2012 'A' Level results came out:

> And, for those completing their UCAS forms this autumn, the government has obliged universities to make key information available for every course. This includes figures on employment outcomes, living costs and contact time. We expect third party organisations, like *Which*, to repackage this information in innovative and accessible ways.
>
> (Willetts, 2012)

Professional opinion is divided about the intentions, the rationality and the viability of these intentions. Data war is likely, over-interpretation of partial information is certain, and institutional gamesmanship will continue in this as in other related promotional zones.

However a start has been made. On contact time the Higher Education Policy Institute (HEPI) has published a series of rangefinding reports (HEPI, 2005, 2006b, 2007, 2009, 2012). In 2013 they were joined by *Which?* (Which, 2013). The National Student Survey (NSS) is now in its eighth year (see website), asking questions about eight key elements of the student experience: teaching, assessment, and feedback, academic support, organization and management, learning resources, personal development, overall satisfaction, and the Students' Union (Association, or Guild). The government is also now requiring institutions to publish for each course 'key information sets' (KIS): student satisfaction, graduate salaries, graduate destinations,

the fee, cost of living, time in class, assessment methods, language of instruction (e.g. Welsh), and satisfaction with the Students' Union. They have produced a mocked-up version (see website).

Globally, we are going through a neo-liberal phase at the moment where human capital and personal economic returns apparently rule: essentially 'learning to earn'. Getting a job will always loom large as a validation of the higher education experience. The Freshman Survey from UCLA's Higher Education Research Institute shows the trend: 'in 1976 about two-thirds of freshmen said the ability to get a job was a very important reason to go to college; in 2012, an all-time high of 88 per cent said so' (Sander, 2013). This certainly underwrites much of the dialogue in the UK and elsewhere about fees and sharing the costs of HE with its eventual beneficiaries.

It is true that the value of higher education in economic terms is substantial, both to the individual, in terms of higher earnings, and to society as a whole. However, we must be careful with this line of argument: higher education does not always provide economic benefit for all individuals. In recent years the supply of graduates has increased dramatically and the wage premium earned by some new graduates appears to be falling (even if surprisingly slowly [see London Economics, 2013]). If, after the present constriction, we resume expansion towards 50 per cent participation by each age cohort, we are likely to see further falls in the personal economic value of a degree. We can already observe substantial diversity in terms of graduates' economic outcomes. For instance, the rate of return to a degree varies by institution, with a higher wage premium for graduates from 'elite' institutions. The value of degrees also varies hugely by subject, with quantitative degrees and some vocationally oriented degrees having greater value. It is important that students are well informed of these nuances of the graduate labour market.

But there is another perspective. Non-financial benefits to higher education also need to be taken into account. The Wider Benefits of Learning Group (WBL) at the Institute of Education has demonstrated on the basis of serious longitudinal study (of cohorts born in 1958, 1970, and now 2000) that participants in HE in the UK are likely to be happier, healthier, and more democratically tolerant (Schuller *et al.*, 2004; Feinstein *et al.*, 2008). There are inter-generational benefits from education too. Graduates are also capable of passing the benefit on (as the study of the Millennium cohort already shows: graduates read to their children).

There is a further issue: colloquially referred to as 'drop-out'. The UK system seems to give the lie to the American presumption that some HE is better than none: those who commence HE and then drop out fall behind economically as compared to their peers who never started. Further, evidence indicates that students from more deprived backgrounds are more likely to drop out even if they are equally qualified when they enter HE. As we expand HE therefore, retention and completion are as important as widening participation.

A related trap is to underestimate the role of students in moulding 'their' higher education. This is partly about choice of subjects, where reports have underlined the difficulties providers have faced (more successfully in recent years) in adjusting to the popularity and unpopularity of certain courses. For example, the 'Media Studies' vogue in a deeply ironic way was a *demand*-led phenomenon (it is ironic, because one of the chief charges is that HE does not respond to demand). The decline in sciences (other than the biosciences) and technology may be irreversible (and we have shielded ourselves from its full effects in the UK because of overseas recruitment). Culture seems to be having an effect here too. A report from the Nuffield Foundation points to a negative correlation between the objective 'development' of societies and enthusiasm of young people for science and technology (in other words it is not just a western disease) (Nuffield Foundation, 2008).

Thirdly there is the question of HE as a *positional good*. The really serious issue raised by HE expansion is about polarization: about the growing gap between those with access to this good, and those without. Expansion of higher education has been demonstrated as a necessary but not sufficient condition of widening participation, and hence greater 'fairness'. When it has been restricted, it has had a disproportionately negative effect on 'non-standard' participation; and in today's policy environment this is likely to happen again. However, as provision expands it increases the gap between the life chances of those who participate and those who do not. We need to look at non-participation at least as much as participation, and to care about disengagement (and re-engagement) at least as much as at recruitment and retention. It seems to be especially difficult to increase lower socio-economic group participation as a proportion, although there has been some modest progress recently and, of course, expansion means that despite this, it will probably increase in absolute terms.

At the heart of the positional matter is the question of *social mobility*. Is higher education participation essentially a shield against downward social mobility for dull middle class children? We do not have any really secure comparative data on this, but a bold attempt at such an analysis has been made by the Sutton Trust (Blanden *et al.*, 2005). It shows how some of the most fully expanded systems (such as the USA) have the lowest levels of intergenerational mobility. Similarly, a celebrated fifteen-country study by Yossi Shavit and others discovered a pattern of 'persistent inequality' even as systems expanded (Shavit *et al.*, 2007: 29).

This debate can all too easily descend into a competition between two narratives: one stressing the role of HE in reproducing patterns of elite formation; the other more confident about the effect of expanded, more democratic systems in enabling new entrants. A fascinating new study by Gareth Williams and Rania Filippakou (making use of a century of data from *Who's Who*) shows how in the UK both narratives can be true. The stranglehold of the ancient universities of Oxford and Cambridge over entry to a variety of elite careers endures. However, at the same time the contribution of the rest of the system (and of those with higher education credentials from overseas) has begun seriously to have an impact (Williams and Filippakou, 2010).

This example of two narratives (the inhibition and the enhancement of social mobility) – each of which can be empirically validated – echoes some other domains covered in this book: like the two routes through American higher education (covered in Chapter 4) or the co-existence of liberal and instrumental course and life choices by students (in Chapter 3). Suman Berry is Chief Economist of Shell, and thus the inheritor of the pioneering work on scenarios of Pierre Wack and others. He describes how his team always works on two scenarios rather than three (or more); it is because, given the chance the participants in any exercise will largely converge on the central idea (personal conversation, January 2013). As several features of higher education confirm, the danger of this kind of thinking is that sometimes both of two contending narratives can be true, and can co-exist in a way that makes no sense of any 'averaging' around a centre that may not exist.

The lazy term of art for the privilege of progression is meritocracy. As Charles Lovelace of the Morehead-Cain Foundation says of the students applying to his organization for scholarships at the University of North Carolina, the challenge is 'how we separate merit from privilege, because so much of what happens to these kids is the result of their privilege rather than their achievement and their motivation' (Hoover, 2013). In this context, it is important to remember that in *The Rise of the Meritocracy* (1958) Michael Young used the term as a warning – not as a goal to be achieved. As he later put it:

> It is good sense to appoint individual people to jobs on their merit. It is the opposite when those who are judged to have merit of a particular kind harden into a new class without room in it for others. ... A social revolution has been accomplished by harnessing schools and universities to the task of sieving people according to education's narrow band of values.
>
> (M. Young, 2001)

Finally, the *historical perspective* is vital.

This is, of course, a tough time to graduate, whether you are about to join, to return to, or to continue within the job market. For today's graduates we have the cumulative effect of: the credit crunch; a palpable loss of confidence in political leadership; ethnic, religious, political, and economic tension all around the world; and, not least, concerns about the future viability of our planet as a home for the human race.

Today's students and recent graduates may think that everything is stacked against them. But I am a historian, and on some, but not all, of these variables we have been here before. I started my degree in 1968 and graduated in 1971.

I arrived in my university in the aftermath of the assassinations of Martin Luther King and Robert Kennedy, and the crushing of the uprising in Czechoslovakia. British troops were sent (back) to Northern Ireland in August 1969. The Berlin Wall was a brooding presence – and nobody predicted how rapidly it would be torn down in 1989. I graduated just before the Oil Crisis, the 'three-day week' and Watergate. The next few years created the circumstances in which Margaret Thatcher's revolution of 1979 became possible, including our large loan from the International Monetary Fund and the 'winter of discontent'.

The big economic differences between my experience and that of today's graduates were, of course, debt and inflation. Individual graduate debt was rare, and rampant inflation acted to wipe it away. Read Margaret Atwood's wonderful little book *Payback* for a comparison with today. According to Atwood, 'we seem to be entering a period in which debt has passed through its most recent harmless and fashionable period, and is reverting to being sinful'. She reports a friend as saying 'debt is the new fat' (Atwood, 2008: 41). Western student bodies caught the wave, and may be left up the beach.

> I'm told that university students tell tales about their ballooning student loans with rueful grins rather than with floods of despairing tears. Everyone's in debt – so what? That's the way it is, and how else are they supposed to get through school? As for paying it all off, they'll think about that later.
>
> (Ibid. 131)

The current political and economic obsession is with graduate 'employability'. It is hard to see how universities can ever win in the 'employability' arena. Most of the things that those outside the academy say they should be supplying in terms of education and training are not only out of the higher education institutions' control, but also poorly understood and ideologically loaded.

Universities cannot create jobs, except indirectly, over longish time scales, and in favourable conditions. Politicians can promote unrealistic ideas about what the employment market actually offers (for example, a significant number of high quality positions in science and technology). Employers are habitual authors of lists of desirable graduate attributes, or more regularly and negatively, of lists of things they say newly employed graduates cannot do (I have included one such at the end of Chapter 4). Meanwhile they continue regularly to screen institutions for potential recruits not on the basis of whether or not the latter have taught these things in specific courses, but more on the perceived reputation of the institution as a whole. (As set out in the Preface, students understand this fact of life, and act – if they can – accordingly.)

All of these tensions are heightened by the constraints of the external economic environment, not least in the context of the global downturn of 2008.

Youth unemployment is now a global phenomenon and, set against the emergence of genuinely mass high education, is bound to have led to the widespread experience not only of graduate unemployment, but also of graduate *under*-employment (and serious displacement by better qualified people of those expecting to take lower status, and generally unskilled jobs).

In these circumstances there are hard questions about what a graduate job is anyway (other than any job taken by a graduate), while even in more prosperous times there are contested issues about whether higher-level skills represent a 'push' or a 'pull' effect.

The good news is that – in general, and again over time – students and graduates seem to have the capacity to make better sense of some of these ley lines than those who purport to speak (or to legislate for them). As mentioned above, the approximately 130,000 subjects of the Higher Education Careers Support Unit (HECSU) Futuretrack survey graduated into the full horrors of the UK economic mess that was initiated by the fall of Northern Rock and went global through the meltdown of Lehman Brothers. If any generation of British graduates could be said to have been let down by those projecting and advising on their futures, they would be it.

However, as demonstrated in the latest sweep (number 4, in 2011/12; the first subjects of the survey enrolled in 2005 and 2006) they appear to have reacted with equanimity, self-awareness, and residual optimism. Although one in ten (of a residual 17,000 respondents) had experienced significant spells of unemployment and four in ten were employed in jobs regarded as 'non-graduate' by traditional classifications (where, interestingly, they were likely to be paid more than non-graduates – perhaps giving some credence to the theory of 'growing the job'), over six in ten were broadly satisfied with their careers to date (about three in ten especially so), and most tellingly, 96 per cent said that given the choice they would 'do it all again' (Futuretrack, 2012: xv–xxix and 195–201). The veteran American television journalist Tom Brokaw shares this positive view of the millennial generation (born, like the Futuretrackers in the last two decades of the twentieth century): 'He calls them the Wary Generation, and he thinks their cautiousness in life decisions is a smart response to their world' (Stein, 2013: 35).

Intergenerational justice

We also need to reflect on how relations *between* the generations have changed. Some authorities (including the current UK Universities Minister) see this as fundamentally a question of intergenerational accounting: the baby-boomers (born into a different type of austerity, after World War II) have stolen the inheritance of Generation X (Willetts, 2011). Others focus on the cultural questions: young people (especially in the Western world) are growing up both faster (in terms of independence and the right to a point of view) and more slowly (in terms of extended economic dependence).

Across Europe ideas about the appropriate age for various transitions in life stages vary significantly but are generally increasing (see the European Social Survey [ESS] website). For example in 2010 the age at which it is considered too old to be living with your parents in Spain was considered to be 31.2 for men and 30.7 for women, and in the UK 29.1 and 28.5 respectively. In 2012 the *Guardian* reported a survey from the insurance company Aviva indicating that families could now expect their student offspring to stay in the family home for an average of a further three years after graduation: shock-horror for the baby-boomers (*The Guardian: Family*, 25 August 2012).

This leads on to a notion of extended adolescence, and a debate about who in fact defines adulthood. Keri Facer, in particular, has been critical of notions that IT fluency is an exclusive attribute of the young (the 'cyber-kid'), that it is possible for their elders to 'manage' this, and that future adulthood should be conceptualized exclusively by those who are already adults. Her solution is 'an education for intergenerational solidarity':

> [I]n conditions of rapid technological development, no generation has a monopoly on expertise or understanding and ... the need to learn, try things out and change is a property now of all age groups. If our urgent challenge is to learn to live well in changing socio-technical environments, we need to draw upon the expertise of all age groups to do so.
>
> (Facer, 2011: 40–2)

A profound influence is thus the developing relationships between students of various types and those who are responsible for designing their academic and professional experience. Alongside the horizontal, or synchronic, tensions and dilemmas raised by external and internal pressures, universities also face a vertical, or diachronic, challenge arising from the relations between the generations. This is the theme of Heller and D'Ambrosio's *Generational Shockwaves* (2008).

This volume has caught a theme about which the consensus is that it is both important and insufficiently understood. In due course 'generational fracture' may recede into the list of HE management themes that have been shown to be too simplistic and ideologically loaded to be of any real use to either scholars or practitioners, like 'new managerialism', 'the management of change', 'income diversification', or 'world-classness' (see the Preface, above). For the moment it has legs.

The basic framework is set by Don Heller: the 'Baby Boomers ... born as World War II was coming to a close' and now 'near retirement'; 'Generation X ... born largely in the 1960s and 1970s', many of whom have become the younger cohort of faculty who are now helping to teach the Millennial Generation of students, those born since 1980' (Heller and D'Ambrosio, 2008: 1). More broadly, the authors consider the contribution to higher education of the six generations of Americans who are alive today: before the 'Boomers' there were the 'GI generation' (born 1901–24) and the 'Silent Generation' (1925–42). The chief merit of this approach is that it brings together in one place consideration of stratigraphic change of both the student and the staff bodies. Work-related hang-ups of teachers and other staff confront the sometimes similar but often different preferences of students. At the moment most of the dilemmas are being played out in the arena of information and communications technologies (ICT). Here on one level 'the faculty sometimes lag behind their students in technological prowess' (Ibid: 64); on another, technologically adept faculty can be frustrated by how superficial and easily satisfied their charges can be (a particularly valuable chapter explores these issues in terms of postgraduate study; it is no longer just about 18-year-old university entrants). It is surprising how rare an exercise this juxtaposition of the 'lived worlds' of the teachers and the taught is in the conventional higher educational literature.

Cultural historians are sceptical about generational tags, but they use them all of the time. The trick is to combine 'internal' (mainly demographic) characteristics with 'external' (mainly 'world-historical') events. Thus in the USA the secular effects of wars – World War II, Korea, Vietnam, and Iraq (and their aftermath – especially in the generous educational support of the GI bill, which probably did more than anything else to democratize American higher education) – are punctuated by crises like the Cuban Missiles, Sputnik, and 9/11 in terms of generational sensibility. Other contemporary contextual features include a more self-consciously diverse, economically beleaguered as well as litigious society (see Baggini, 2008: 27).

The dangers include stereotyping and a failure to recognize elements of continuity alongside those of change. More than one author in *Generational Shockwave* uses the metaphor of a multi-stranded rope in order to try to understand what is going on (Heller and D'Ambrosio, 2008: 60, 158). The dynamics of the parent–child relationship are particularly important as the former seek to re-balance where they think they went wrong and the latter both rebel against and seek to please their parents (it was Jung who talked about children enacting the 'unlived lives' of their parents). Universities can be caught in the middle, as they always have been. As one set of witnesses here suggests: 'to see how any age bracket is likely to transform in the decades ahead, don't look at the set of people who currently occupy that bracket – look down the ladder at the next generation due to pass through it' (Ibid: 15).

One major impression given by this analysis – despite all sorts of attempts to downplay it (not least because of the age and status of the authors) – is about the current, continuing power of the 'Boomer' generation, representing the largest birth cohort ever in the history of the United States. They have largely created the present system, and they are hanging on to it as (after a huge fight) mandatory retirement has become illegal. The United States differs from the UK in that its average age of teaching staff is higher, and increasing (currently 54, as opposed to 43, Ibid. 139–40). Equally important, the next generation will have to sustain them through an unprecedented length of retirement, in good and ill health. Indeed, demography is one of the most influential moulders of a higher education system, with stark differences between the adjustments and pressures felt by those nations and regions with rising and those with declining proportions of young people.

Ironically families of students are becoming more salient in terms of educational choices, economic aspirations, and student support at a time when public policy is loading more of the longer-term costs on students than on their parents. In the North and West, the American 'College Fund' is receding as a model, while more and more parents are participating in open days, overseeing college applications and intervening (sometimes litigiously) to ensure that their investment is sound. Parents are generally more concerned about long-term debt than the children (and graduates) against whom it is being charged. In Asia, Simon Marginson has meanwhile (and somewhat contentiously) outlined a 'Confucian' model of higher education, in which family investment in the future – through their graduate offspring – is central:

> The essential cultural condition is Confucian values. These values run as deep as classical civilisation or the Judeo-Christian ethic in the West. In the Confucian world, the project of self-cultivation via education is joined to filial duty and the honour of the ancestral line. Success in and through education lodges the family more securely in space and time.
>
> (Marginson, 2010)

In China, as economic growth slows but the higher education participation rate continues to climb, severe structural problems are arising, not least for the children of whom so much is expected by their families. In major cities under and unemployed graduates have become known as the 'ant people' (Jennings, 2010). A survey undertaken by Chengdu's Southwestern University of Finance and Economics in early 2013 showed the urban unemployment rate for graduates running at twice the level (16.8 per cent) of those with only high school qualifications (8.2 per cent), with evidence of widespread reluctance of young graduates (many still supported by their families) to take on apparently 'demeaning' work (Bradsher, 2013). Meanwhile youth unemployment – especially across Europe (and less well documented in the so-called 'Arab Spring' states) – is a major structural problem for today's economy and society. In late 2012 Eurostat (the statistical office of the European Union) reported that:

> in September 2012, the youth unemployment rate was 22.8 per cent in the EU27 and 23.3 per cent in the euro area, compared with 21.7 per cent and 21.0 per cent respectively in September 2011. In September 2012 the lowest rates were observed in Germany (8.0 per cent), the Netherlands

(9.7 per cent) and Austria (9.9 per cent), and the highest in Greece (55.6 per cent in July 2012) and Spain (54.2 per cent).

(see website)

As companies hoard labour in response to the financial crisis a vicious circle is stimulated, of fewer jobs, of cohorts of graduating students 'stacking up', of unpaid work experience (including the contentious 'internships') only being practically available to members of well-off families, the displacement effect of relatively unskilled jobs being taken by the highly educated (sometimes termed 'under-employment' – an impending global dilemma [see Brown *et al.*, 2011]), and the revival of political activism described in the last chapter.

Against this cycle of despair, Richard Sennett's is a principled voice of protest: 'what galls me about the current situation is that a structural problem of capitalism has been dumped into the lives of young people as their personal problem'. He describes how many groups respond, not simply by complaint, but also by action, including willingness – often at social cost – to be mobile ('emigration'), accepting whatever is available in the 'flexible' work market (he calls this the 'night anchor'), and by accepting self-employment as a positive way forward (the 'start-up') (Sennett, 2012a). Guy Standing has recently used the term 'precariat' to characterize a group into which these graduates could be said to descend easily: '[its members] live and work insecurely, flitting between short-term dead-end jobs, without an occupational identity or opportunity to develop themselves. Many are overqualified for the jobs they are expected to take' (Standing, 2012). Interestingly, however, higher education can at least help with identity. Sennett adds his weight to the liberal revival described above (in Chapter 3), when he talks about the 'misplaced specificity' of much of today's undergraduate education:

> We would do much better to provide young people with intellectual challenge and depth – which is what universities are properly about. The number of jobs would not thereby increase; the integrity of the academic enterprise would.
>
> (Sennett, 2012a)

One of the tensions in this story is about whether employability is more or less than capability – to survive, thrive, and serve in the modern world.

Chapter 7

Higher education membership: Terms and conditions

This chapter returns to the question of 'transformation', through some contemporary witnesses. It proceeds to an account of the psychological and moral 'contract' implied by participation in modern university life.

'Transformation' claims: Ten voices

Most of the claims about the purposes and achievements of higher education are irreducibly individualistic: it will change your life, through conversion or confirmation of faith, by improving your character, by giving you marketable 'abilities', by making you a better member of the community, or by simply being 'capable' of operating more effectively in the contemporary world. The Singaporean student Hongjun Wang has captured this flavour with his successful website and spin-off activities under the banner 'The Art of Taking Personal Responsibility' (TAOTPR – see website). However, the picture is more complicated. All of these qualities scale up, but in differing ways.

There follow some contemporary British (and two American) voices, from inside and outside what might be called the 'establishment'. Each offers a singular or a multiple perspective on the ten transformation claims set out in Chapter 1.

Here we have personal development, social engagement, networks, and love of subject from the Chief Executive of the Office of the Independent Adjudicator:

> University was my entry into the world in all its aspects. I found out how to study, how to listen, and how to be tolerant. I made lifelong friends and was fortunate to have some wonderful teachers.
>
> (Behrens, 2010)

The noted comedian David Mitchell reflects on maturation and protected time:

> Except in the case of a few very vocational degrees, university isn't about what you learn on the course, it's about how that learning, how living and studying somewhere new, changes the way you think and who you are. Instead of forcing kids to make binding career choices at 17, higher education is supposed to give kids who would benefit from further academic development a bit of space in which to find themselves.
>
> (Mitchell, 2010)

David Watson

A slightly more cynical, but none the less positive view, from the journalist Peter Barkham:

> I always felt that I did not quite belong at the university. But that didn't matter: Cambridge still bequeathed me a key to the British establishment. In just 72 weeks of study, I was more profoundly transformed than I could have ever expected. By the time I graduated, gothic halls no longer intimidated me; nor did walking into an oak-panelled room full of folk in dinner jackets; nor did small talk with drunk rugby players destined for a job in their uncle's merchant bank. I didn't feel chippy or cowed by anything, any one or any job. Perhaps foolishly, I felt well-educated.
>
> (Barkham, 2010)

This is another journalist, Tom Utley of the *Daily Mail*, changing his mind about advising his son not to go to university:

> I've long been one of those irritating people – mostly graduates, I notice, since those without degrees tend to attach much greater value to them – who believe that too many young people go to universities these days, while for many of them it's a waste of time and money.
>
> With that thought in mind, I steeled myself for the worst last week, preparing comforting words for my youngest if he failed to get his grades. It wasn't the end of the world, I was going to tell him. University really wasn't all it's cracked up to be – and it was certainly not a guaranteed passport to wealth. Just look at his two older brothers.
>
> And yet, reader, he passed!
>
> And as soon as he broke the news that he'd achieved the grades he needed to get into Sheffield to read Spanish – and, yes, history – my heart fair burst with pride and happiness.
>
> Suddenly, the joy of my three years at university flooded back to me. I realized that in countless intangible ways, those seemingly wasted years were the most hugely enriching time of my life – and that everything I'd been planning to tell the boy was rubbish.
>
> To those who see a degree course as a path to making money, I would still advise caution – especially after the fees go up next year. And anyone considering some of the vaguer-sounding courses on offer, such as community development or social welfare, might do well to check the drop-out rates before starting to run up those massive loans.
>
> But even if you forget the lot, you just can't put a price on three or four years at a proper university, studying a proper subject such as history. And don't believe any world-weary old fool who tells you otherwise.
>
> (Utley, 2011)

The following is the official 'portmanteau' view, from the *Browne Report*. You can find nine of my ten claims here – religion is missing (unless it is implied by 'community'):

Higher Education matters because it transforms the lives of individuals. On graduating, graduates are more likely to be employed, more likely to enjoy higher wages and better job satisfaction, and more likely to find it easier to move from one job to another. Participating in higher education enables individuals from low income backgrounds and then their families to enter higher status jobs and increase their earnings. Graduates enjoy substantial health benefits – a reduced likelihood of smoking, and lower incidence of obesity and depression. They are less likely to be involved in crime, more likely to be actively engaged with their children's education and more likely to be active in their communities.

(IRHEFSF, 2010: 14)

Here are two contrasting voices from the United States, the first from a distinguished Princeton literature professor and the second from a renowned historian at Notre Dame, America's premier Catholic university:

American higher education is a system that is messy, reduplicative, unfair – just like American Society as a whole – but it has made genuine commitments to equality and to a greater degree of social justice, to the extent that it is within its control, than most other institutions of the society.

(Brooks, 2011)

There are only two worthwhile objectives for everything we do, in the university and out of it: enhancing life and preparing for death. No institution needs a more detailed mission statement than that, as long as the people in it think about what it means.

(Fernández-Armesto, 2011)

Religion makes a comeback (as if often does in the USA). The potential university strapline – 'enhancing life and preparing for death' – is eerily reminiscent of Zadie Smith's philosophy department quoted in Chapter 6.

Sometimes the tone is unashamedly nostalgic. This is the view from All Souls and the Council for the Defence of British Universities (CDBU), launched on 13 November 2012:

We are all deeply anxious about the future of British universities. Our list of concerns is a long one. It includes the discontinuance of free university education; the withdrawal of direct public funding for the teaching of the humanities and the social sciences; the subjection of universities to an intrusive regime of government regulation and inquisitorial audit; the crude attempt to measure and increase scholarly 'output'; the requirement that all academic research have an 'impact' on the economy; the transformation of self-governing communities of scholars into mega-businesses, staffed by a highly paid executive class, who oversee the professors, or middle managers, who in turn rule over an ill-paid and often temporary or part-time proletariat of junior lecturers and research assistants, coping with an ever worsening staff–student ratio; the notion that universities, rather than collaborating in their common task, should compete with one another, and with private providers, to sell their services in a market, where students are seen, not as partners in a joint enterprise of learning and understanding, but as 'consumers', seeking the cheapest deals that will enable them to emerge with the highest earning prospects; the indiscriminate application of the label 'university' to institutions whose primary task is to provide vocational training and whose staff do not carry out research; and the rejection of the idea that higher education might have a non-monetary value, or that science, scholarship and intellectual inquiry are important for reasons unconnected with economic growth.

What a contrast with the medieval idea that knowledge was a gift of God, which was not to be sold for money, but should be freely imparted. Or with the nineteenth-century German concept of the university devoted to the higher learning; or with the tradition in this country that some graduates, rather than rushing off to Canary Wharf, might wish to put what they had learned to the service of society by teaching in secondary schools or working for charities or arts organizations or nature conservation or foreign aid agencies or innumerable other good but distinctly unremunerative causes.

(Thomas, 2012)

Here is a succinct statement of what Thomas is complaining about, from the Director of policy and research at the Chartered Management Institute:

University is becoming less about traditional student experiences and more about getting the most out of an education to secure a job.

(Wilton, 2011–12)

It is important that all of these statements are made by and on behalf of 'insiders', that is participants and prospective participants. It is also significant that, by and large, the positive accounts have survived the transition from so-called 'elite' to 'mass' higher education. As a larger proportion of the population has a 'stake' in higher education – including vicariously through their children – they are more likely to view it positively. That is why 'college' has retained its upbeat reference in American popular culture, including through hard times.

In contrast in England, with the increase in the participation rate stalled (while other countries race past 'mass' to 'universal' higher education in Martin Trow's sadly elegiac view of the world), there are still influential voices that view higher education with a mixture of envy and contempt (Trow, 1974). Here, for example, is Auberon Waugh, son of Evelyn (the creator in *Brideshead Revisited* [1945] of one of the most sensuous evocations of the elite university past) writing in 1975, just before the UK followed the US in almost quadrupling the age participation rate. Incidentally the younger Waugh crashed out of Christ Church, Oxford, after just one year:

> Hatred of students stretches across the whole political spectrum, through every age group and social class, and I often wonder why no politician has thought of harnessing it to his own ends … The traditional explanation for working-class hatred of students was that they outraged ordinary social values: they didn't work. … Next there was an element of implied superiority: man is born equal but some of them pass their O levels and some don't … Finally, of course, there was and remains the element of sexual jealousy which may always have existed between the generations but is made particularly bitter nowadays by the apparently endless sexual opportunities available to young people. Something we never knew … Ingratitude, idleness, lust, hypocrisy, and self-righteousness are the main characteristics of this cancer in our midst which we call higher education.
>
> Auberon Waugh, 'Hatred of Students', *New Statesman*, 1975
> (reprinted in Cook, 2010: 32–3)

We should not, however, think that assessments like this died with Auberon Waugh. This is John Walsh of the *Independent* railing against the prospect of a Higher Education Achievement Record (HEAR) in late 2012:

> No longer will students emerge from their three years of hoggish indolence, erotic experiment and cyberspatial plagiarism with a First, a Second or a Third. They'll now be given a Higher Education Achievement Report, which is like a school report, only longer and far more boring.
>
> (Walsh, 2012)

Standing back, these statements, collectively, raise a number of complex questions:

Does initial (or undergraduate) higher education invariably change the lives of those who participate in it? If so – for example in economic or moral terms, or in any other way – how? And if so, why? Who or what is responsible for bringing this about? Are these effects serendipitous or predictable, designed or accidental, desired or feared?

Is higher education a necessary or even a sufficient condition for any such 'transformations', as they are fashionably called today? Are they more general aspects of maturation for some people? Could HE, indeed, act to inhibit or delay such development for others?

Can all varieties of modern higher education make similar claims? It may perhaps be no accident that the first three of my introductory voices benefitted from the kind of higher education that Michael Oakeshott memorably (and perhaps now anachronistically) called in 1950 'the gift of an interval':

> A man may at any time of his life begin to explore a new branch of learning or engage in fresh activity, but only at a university may he do this without a rearrangement of his scarce resources of time and energy; in later life he is committed to so much that he cannot easily throw off. The characteristic gift of a university is the gift of an interval. Here is an opportunity to put aside the hot allegiances of youth without the necessity of at once acquiring new loyalties to take their place. Here is a break in the tyrannical course of irreparable events; a period in which to look around on the world and upon oneself without the sense of an enemy at one's back or the insistent pressure to make up one's mind; a moment in which to taste the mystery without the necessity of at once seeking a solution.
>
> (Oakeshott, 1989: 113–14)

At the same time, universities are institutionally in the 'knowledge' business. The university is probably the most significant institution in both the historical and contemporary processes of creating, testing, applying, and evaluating all aspects of knowledge. As Louis Menand puts the point in his *The Marketplace of Ideas*:

> Knowledge is our most important business. The success of almost all our other business depends on it, but its value is not only economic. The pursuit, production, dissemination, application, and preservation of knowledge are the central activities of a civilization. Knowledge is social memory, a connection to the past; and it is social hope, an investment in the future. The ability to create knowledge and put it to use is *the* adaptive characteristic of humans.
>
> (Menand, 2010: 13)

Universities are distinctive in that they deal in a non-dogmatic, open and experimental way with both 'social memory' and 'social hope'.

In similar vein, another distinguished American commentator, Andrew Delbanco identifies the five 'habits of thought and feeling' that are essential for students 'trying to cross that treacherous terrain on their way toward self-knowledge'. They are:

- A sceptical discontent with the present, informed by a sense of the past.
- The ability to make connections among seemingly disparate phenomena.

- Appreciation of the natural world, enhanced by knowledge of science and the arts.
- A willingness to imagine experience from perspectives other than one's own.
- A sense of ethical responsibility.

(Delbanco, 2012: 5–6)

The university 'oath': Ten commandments

In the course of this book, I have given a very fluid picture of the intentions of universities, as set out in their founding conditions and their rationalization for teaching and learning in higher education. I have also tried to suggest how some of the dilemmas that emerge (chiefly about the 'transformation' hypothesis) might be approached. Essentially, this leads on to the question of what is enduring in the enterprise, especially after the watershed of the Enlightenment has been crossed.

As a contribution to the debate, I have attempted to scope out what the ten commandments given to a contemporary higher education institution (I am not sure by whom) might be (Watson, 2007: 101–6; 2009, 122–9). Essentially this analysis extends the work of Eric Ashby and Northrop Frye on 'the educational contract' (Ashby, 1969; Frye, 1967: 1). Each of these injunctions carries with it a set of dilemmas, both philosophical and practical:

1. Strive to tell the truth.
'Academic freedom', in the sense of following difficult ideas wherever they may lead, is possibly the fundamental 'academic' value.

The UK Education Reform Act of 1988 is often cited as a legislative guarantee of academic freedom. After very heavy lobbying, especially in the House of Lords, it was declared that faculty jobs should not be threatened when they 'put forward new ideas and controversial and unpopular opinions' (Education Reform Act, 1988: 202[2]). However, professional observers mostly look to the United States as a test bed for the construction and defence of academic freedom. Some of the most eloquent formal definitions were established here, notably by the American Association of University Professors (AAUP) in 1915 as follows: 'freedom of inquiry and research; freedom of teaching within the university or college; and freedom of extra-mural utterance and action' (Gerstmann and Streb, 2006: ix). Moreover, America has seen these principles severely tested, notably in the late nineteenth and early twentieth century flexing of industrial muscle and in the anti-communist witch-hunts of the McCarthy era. Another contentious area has been government's direct and indirect governance of science (and of scientists).

Today there is a sense that such trials are being visited upon the academic community again; in the context of national (or homeland) security hysteria, neo-conservative foreign policy, corporate muscle (again), and internet-enabled monitoring and exposure of professorial opinion (to say nothing of general funding pressures and the atrophy of tenure). The more sophisticated American commentators, however, acknowledge the limited sense in which this is so: the barbarians are still basically on the other side of the gates, and things are much worse elsewhere (Ibid. 42–60). Meanwhile non-American historians of the culture and society of the United States know that the country can from time to time exhibit its best and its worst self. The 14th Amendment to the Constitution, which was designed to ensure equality for former slaves and their descendants, degenerated into a licence for abuse by private corporations ('persons' in law) at the turn of the twentieth century. Conversely, almost all sophisticated observers knew that as a result of the peculiar institution of the detention centre at Guantanamo Bay, the then President George W. Bush would end up in the Supreme Court, and that he would lose (as he did in Hamdan vs. Rumsfield in 2006).

It is also important to acknowledge that the privileges as well as the responsibilities associated with academic freedom belong to all members of the community, including students (Macfarlane, 2012). Academic freedom is in one sense synonymous with 'free speech', but it includes some additional strictures. It is also about disciplined speech. This is what connects the commandments about truth-seeking with those about good behaviour inside the academy.

The main practical dilemma relates to institutional *autonomy*, seen, for example by the signatories of the *Magna Charta Universitatum* on the 900th anniversary of the foundation of the University of Bologna in 1988, as the essence of what the modern university is and how it works (Lay, 2004: 109). Reflecting on this assertion in 2012, Peter Scott entered a cautionary note: 'the evidence suggest that academic freedom has always been conditional – and, to a large extent, contingent on the 'success' of the university in satisfying political goals, social aspirations and economic demands' (Scott, 2012: 6). None the less, the Humboldtian idea of a university that can operate in 'freedom and loneliness' remains powerful and evocative (Watson, 2009: 78).

2. Take care in establishing the truth

Adherence to scientific method is critical here (as in the use of evidence, and 'falsifiability' principle), but so too is the concept of social scientific 'warrant', and the search for 'authenticity' in the humanities and arts.

Universities provide the most obvious arena for playing out the age-old battle between what C.P. Snow called in 1959 (in his Rede Lecture at Cambridge) the 'two cultures'. At that stage the battle lines were drawn, between those who could state the Second Law of Thermodynamics and those who had read a work of Shakespeare (Snow, 1959: 3). English schoolchildren had in many cases been forced to choose between these sides very early in their secondary education. This, at least, has improved, with most 16-year-olds doing some systematic study from each camp through their GCSEs, despite the continuing over-specialization in the country of both upper secondary education and presentation for university entrance.

Stereotypes endure, and take on the trappings of their contemporary champions and critics. Today, you would probably want to contrast Henderson's *The Geek Manifesto* with Nussbaum's *Not for Profit* (Henderson, 2012; Nussbaum, 2010). But there are also signs of *rapprochement*. Modern students, scholars, and practitioners are throwing ropes across the divide. Many of these have to do with information and communications technology; others have to do with design; and yet others to do with the sociology of innovation. The late twentieth-century growth of business schools has something to do with this. One result is that in the contemporary Western university the most entrepreneurial students are found not in the faculty of engineering, but in art and design.

Another ambition of liberal higher education is at play here – and it is no accident that the tradition (and some of the parts of comprehensive universities delivering it) is often referred to as 'Arts and Sciences'. In its early twenty-first century guise it combines scientific with cultural literacy, and both in turn with new formulations of older truths like emotional intelligence, sense-making, and capability. It is frequently disparaged by the advocates of what is sometimes called 'scientific fundamentalism', such as Mark Henderson (2012: 76) and Ben Goldacre (2005).

As we look across this disciplinary spectrum, one of the key dilemmas is the borderland between *analysis* and *advocacy*. In science Richard Feynman, as usual, puts the point brilliantly: whenever you have a good idea, your first obligation is to think about everything that might be wrong about it (Feynman, 2005: 360). In social science, both quantitative and qualitative methods have their techniques for assigning significance to apparent discoveries. In the humanities, Stephan Collini has some interesting strictures on professional responsibility. In a powerful essay on 'the character of the humanities' (embedded within his otherwise less well-grounded account of the trials of the contemporary academy – see Chapter 8 below) he talks about the tendency of the technique of critique to lead to a 'hermeneutics of suspicion'. This produces a 'curious asymmetry' in which 'the assumptions of the objects of study are subjected to a more severe regime than are the assumptions of those doing the studying'. The outcome is a humanized version of the Feynman rule, in fact reversing this pathology: 'extend the greatest possible imaginative sympathy to the expressions of the human agents we study, but combine it with the greatest possible scepticism about any of the explanatory mechanisms by means of which we try to account for their action' (Collini, 2012: 83).

One temptation here is commercial. Sir Keith Thomas, chair of the judging panel for the Wolfson History Prize, has recently warned against the early career search for a bestseller, as well as the 'parasitic relationship between higher-profile historians with a flair for language and a publisher, and less eye-catching academics whose diligent efforts in archives and libraries end up by being cited in the books of their more media-savvy colleagues' (Milmo, 2012). These things also count in public life, for which higher education is a much-vaunted preparation. Here, for example, is Andrew Rawnsley's ruthlessly accurate account of Tony Blair in crusading mode: 'Blair was a sincere deceiver. He told the truth about what he believed. He lied about the strength of the evidence for his belief' (Rawnsley: 2010: 121).

It is important to note that this is not an argument against the honourable tradition of rhetoric itself: the systematic art of effective argumentation. This, of course, has a foundational place in the university curriculum, as a component of both the Trivium (with grammar and logic) and preceding the Quadrivium (of arithmetic, geometry, music, and astronomy). As its popular historian Sam Leith states, 'Rhetoric is hustling, and our forefathers knew it. For fifteen centuries or so, the study of rhetoric was at the centre of Western education' (Leith, 2011: 33). Mandatory courses in essay writing in American universities are sometimes called 'Freshman English', but almost equally as regularly 'Rhetoric'. But no part of this distinguished tradition is about making a bad argument or case well.

On the extreme downside, there's a particular type of academic bad faith, which moves too quickly to persuasion in advance of the secure establishment of the grounds for conviction. Will, for example, the Chinese drive for institutions with 'world-class' status be undermined by the evidence about endemic scientific fraud and dishonesty (Jacobs, 2010), or the reports about 'banned' subjects in university classrooms (Farrar, 2013)?

Laziness can be in play, as in the phenomenon of 'gift authorship'. Here the case of Professor Geoffrey Chamberlain, adding his name to a former student's paper in the *British Journal of Obstetrics and Gynaecology* apparently declaring a stunning break through (Malcolm Pearce's claim of a transplanted ectopic pregnancy, subsequently deemed to be fraudulent) is a cautionary tale. There is hubris in the explanation: 'The head of department's name is always put on reports out of politeness. I was not part of this work, but have always trusted Mr Pearce' (Smith, J., 1994). Both academic careers were ruined.

An important backdrop to much of the discussion in this book has been the prevalence of corruption in public and personal life in its special twenty-first-century forms, and as it affects university life. Corruption is the worm in the apple of what I am trying to write about. It actually calls the whole project into question. It influences behaviour at various levels, and they can be mutually reinforcing: students, staff (academic and administrative), teams of various kinds, and institutions corporately (not just in the sense of cultural attitudes, but also in terms of all sorts of practical transactions with the wider world).

There is a danger in assuming that corruption is solely, or largely, a presence in the developing world or 'Global South', connected with the wider abuse of power, the mal-distribution of resources, and the absence of Western-style institutional and professional traditions. This is a mistake: the West, the North, and those systems established in their mould all have problems. The bulk of my stories so far about universities behaving badly have come from the UK and USA. In France, the government has stepped in to take over the management of Sciences-Po, following a highly critical audit (*Economist*, 2012b). In Germany two cabinet ministers have stepped down in 2011 and 2013 because the doctoral theses have been found to be plagiarized (DeSantis, 2013b). This has provoked a national crisis of confidence about first, whether or not German universities can continue to be relied upon as the European 'gold standard', and second, the practice of counting doctoral conferrals in setting funding levels (Hockenos, 2013). In Italy high levels of nepotism are seen as undermining scientific competitiveness (Nowikowski, 2011). In Spain whistle-blowers claim to have exposed widespread networks of research misconduct (Jump, 2012). Dutch higher education has been rocked by the unmasking of the social psychologist Diederik Stapel as a career-long fraud, including in his own autobiography (Stroebe and Hewstone, 2013: 36). Moving to the former Soviet states, greater freedom has either unleashed or exposed massive scandals like procurement in the Ukraine (Abramovych, 2012) or bribery in Georgia (Orkodashvili, 2010). Moving East, professors in prestigious Japanese universities can use the *juku* (crammer) system to increase their income and undermine open admissions (*Economist*, 2011). Moving South, the Israeli government has subverted its rules and procedures on academic approvals to use a military edict to upgrade an institution (Ariel University) on the occupied West Bank (Sherwood, 2012). And so on.

By behaving well (and in particular following this second commandment, to 'take care' with their heartland business) universities should be on the cutting edge of reducing (with a view to eliminating) corruption. It is always possible, however, for this drive to slip back into the maelstrom of individual or group competitive positioning.

3. Be fair

This is about equality of opportunity, non-discrimination, and perhaps even affirmative action. Along with 'freedom' in the academic value-system goes 'respect for persons'. Nussbaum also writes about 'the ability to imagine the experience of another' (Nussbaum, 2010: 10). The relationship between truth-seeking and taking care is analogous to another vital plank of the academic psychological contract, about the interdependence of completion and collaboration. We are engaged in a cut-throat, permanently conflicted enterprise, and yet setting and abiding by the rules of the game are essential for progress.

This is why *attitude* and civility matter, and why universities are natural environments for negotiated speech-codes and the like. They throw up issues where the terms of engagement are critical, like hard (even 'wicked') questions, significant diversity (of people and commitments), a didactic culture, and a necessarily high value on proceduralism.

Veterans of university management – and of its politics – know that perversity is always just around the corner: for example, in the confusion of sincerity and rudeness, and the drive for pyrrhic victories (as when a technical – or procedural – knock-out can be claimed to trump a moral defeat). There are famous examples of when and how this can go wrong, and of art imitating life. To take one such, there is an uncanny similarity between both the substance and the style of Philip Roth's story of the fate of a college dean using what is identified as a racial epithet ('spooks' in *The Human Stain*) and Alan Kors and Harvey Silverglate's account of a similar student case (Roth, 2000: 6). Here it is 'water buffalos' in the equally unrestrained polemic of *The Shadow University* (Kors and Silverglate, 1998: 9–33)

4. Always be ready to explain

Academic freedom is a 'first amendment' and not a 'fifth amendment' right: it is about freedom of speech and not about protection from self-incrimination (Watson, 2000: 85–7). It does not absolve any member of the academic community from the obligation to explain his or her actions, and as far as possible their consequences. *Accountability* is inescapable, and should not be unreasonably resisted. It should also be exercised with care. Academics need to resist the temptation to abuse their authority by expressing definitive views in areas where they know little (it is a law of academic life that they tend to grow in confidence the further they are away from their true fields of expertise). Marcus Aurelius was, as usual, incisive in urging us to treat with respect our power to inform opinions (Watson, 2009: 139, 137). Institutions should take similar care before they unleash on the media their 'expert' spokespersons on this or that.

5. Do no harm

This is where the assessment of consequences cashes out (and presents our nearest equivalent to the Hippocratic oath, to strive 'not to harm but to help'). It is about non-exploitation, either of human subjects, or of the environment. It underpins other notions like 'progressive engagement'. It helps with really wicked issues like the use of animals in medical experiments.

The global scientific consensus is that this resource is essential to the advance of medical science and the safety of procedures. There have, however, been effective moves to 'replace, refine and reduce' the impact to the absolute minimum, resulting for example in the elimination of animal testing for cosmetic and other discretionary projects. The location and use of animal facilities inside and specifically for universities has meanwhile become a lightning rod for protest, including violent episodes and the prosecution of conspirators and protestors. In these circumstances, keeping the temperature down – on both sides – is hard. The unacceptable behaviour of protestors should not be matched by triumphalism and denial on the part of the scientists and their supporters. The company at the heart of the Oxford battles (Huntingdon Life Sciences) has been subject to appalling attacks, on their employees, suppliers, and share-holders. Nevertheless, the record shows that it was their successful prosecution, in 1997, and the revocation of their licence, that sparked much of the current protective legislation (Broughton, 2006). There is something morally questionable about marching in favour of what some would regard as the necessary evil of testing, as has happened in Oxford (Henderson, 2012: 31–2).

The key here is *anticipation*, and careful assessment of consequence, although as with many such injunctions, there are also potential downsides. In a doctoral thesis on Muslim chaplaincies, Aly Kassam-Remtulla has developed the theory of the 'anticipatory university', where the prime motivation is risk aversion rather than risk-taking (Kassam-Remtulla, 2012).

6. Keep your promises

Universities and colleges are involved in a variety of contracts and partnerships. Their record is good: on large-scale projects – on which millions of pounds rest – the examples of the university partner walking away from a done deal are very rare. Meanwhile, the commercial partner can often withdraw, citing changes in strategy, the business cycle, or even changes in management. Such 'business' excuses for retreating from or unreasonably seeking to renegotiate agreements are much less acceptable in an academic context.

There is an element here of truth in *advertising*, not least in terms of the engagement with the undergraduate student market. Analysis of undergraduate prospectuses reveals, for example, the very limited range of claims of distinctive or exceptional performance. These almost always include: a research environment (on a scale from 'intensive' to 'informed'); attention to teaching and learning (much more likely to be about infrastructure – like 'world-class learning resources' – than turning attention to pedagogy itself); graduate destinations (including the ubiquitous 'employability' claim); an 'international' community; and the social and recreational environment (the latter has receded a little lately in favour of the first four – not many lead any more, as they once did, on the quality of the local nightclubs).

7. Respect your colleagues, your students and especially your opponents

Working in an academic community means listening as well as speaking, seeking always to understand the other point of view, and ensuring that rational discourse is not derailed by prejudice, by egotism, or by bullying of any kind. Academic life is inescapably competitive; it also manages this competition through deeply collaborative and mutually supportive structures (peer review, external examining, and so on). Two American university presidents (Barry Glassner of Lewis and Clark, Oregon, and Morton Schapiro of Northwestern) have recently written doubting 'that any CEO, if asked to name his or her greatest challenges, would include on the list what we put near the top: the obligation to create civil communities in an era of incivility' (Glassner and Schapiro, 2013).

Most such control mechanisms are at the level of courses, subjects and professional areas. Institutionally, the competition can all too easily degrade into a kind of *arms race*. For example, the main voluntary interest groups (or 'gangs') rarely make much sense in terms of objective performance. In the UK there are currently five (as follows – numbers are as on websites on 11 November 2012), although the situation is increasingly fluid, and it is very hard to make sense, for example, of the Russell Group on any objective measure:

- The Russell Group of self-proclaimed 'research-intensive' institutions (24)
- The '94 Group of smaller 'research-intensives' (12)
- 'Million+', claiming to educate over a million students and made up chiefly of former polytechnics and Scottish central institutions (21)
- Guild HE – the representative group of pre-1992 Colleges of Higher Education (25)
- The University Alliance – a group formerly called 'non-aligned'! (perhaps better termed the Groucho Marx Group) (25).

In particular, it is clear that institutional status (and 'gang' membership) have very little to do with sound and responsible management, which is found (or not) in all types of institutions. In an attempt to show how specious many of these claimed boundaries are, Brian Ramsden and I created in 2007 the Association of Seaside Universities. We were able to get convincing contributions to our manifesto from all 14 eligible universities (Watson, 2009: 105–13).

8. Sustain the community

All of the values so far expressed are deeply communal. Obligations that arise are not just to the subject or professional community, or even to the institution in which you might be working at any one time, but to the family of institutions that make up the university sector, nationally and internationally. The higher education *ambience* belongs to us all.

9. Guard your treasure

University and college communities, and those responsible for leading and managing them, are in the traditional sense 'stewards' of real and virtual assets, and of the capacity to continue to operate responsibly and effectively. In recent years, public *access* to these resources, facilities and *atmosphere* has been increasingly salient.

As large, influential institutions in Civil Society, universities are inescapably in the heritage business. We store important things on behalf of the community as a whole, and ought to make them available when and how they are needed.

The arrival of mass higher education has coincided (it may have helped to create) a context in which such access is no longer exclusively on the HEI's terms. There are honourable exceptions to this rule. Oxford's Ashmolean Museum is one – founded in 1638, but under Elias Ashmole, formally open to the public from the time of its transfer to Oxford in 1683 (see website). However, it has been the more recent attachment of conditions to planning approvals and funding allocations that has irrevocably ensured that new and remodelled facilities (for sports, recreation and arts) have public use agreements embedded in their design, policies, and management.

10. Never be satisfied

Perhaps this is the academic equivalent of the golden rule. Academic communities understood the principles of 'continuous improvement' long before they were adopted by 'management' literature. At the same time, they are a curious mixture of conformity and non-conformity. As set out in various ways in this account, the higher education enterprise is about initiation and training in ways of thinking and doing. You have to get up to speed to join in the conversation, whether it is sharing a framework of references, or being skilled at procedures (in the library as well as the laboratory), and to understand the problems that are worthy of your fellow travellers' concerns. There is a large element, across the disciplines, of doing what Thomas Kuhn called 'normal science' (Kuhn, 1962). But it is also, from time to time about breaking the moulds, of declaring that the Emperor has no clothes, or starting again.

As a result, academics also understand the merciless and *asymptotic* nature of our business. The academic project will never be complete or perfect. Sometimes this perception is self-serving. Glyn Davis writes about the 'nagging worry' that somehow, somewhere, somebody is doing it better (Davis, 2010: 33). Elaine Showalter quotes the University of Texas professor of gender studies Ann Cvetovic:

> Academe breeds particular forms of panic and anxiety leading to what gets to be called depression – the fear that you have nothing to say, or that you can't say what you want to say, or that you have something to say but it's not important enough or smart enough.
>
> (Showalter, 2013: 4)

This pathology is, of course, shared by the established and the famous. This is Isaiah Berlin, whose public self-confidence was legendary:

> I wish I didn't worry so much myself: worry about not writing books, worry about writing books when I have written them, worry about what people will think, worry about the fact that other people write good books …
>
> (Alberge, 2013)

But at its more principled level the resulting kind of 'professional worrying' is almost Talmudic in its orientation. The truth is there, and we shall strive to discover it, but as we approach we know that it will move away (even the postmodernists can take some satisfaction from this dilemma). Collini again:

> What they (we) are doing much of the time is worrying. The default condition of the scholar is professional dissatisfaction. No matter how exhilarating it may be to discover new evidence or come up with an illuminatingly apt characterization, one can never (and perhaps should

never) entirely banish the sense that the current state of one's work can only ever have the status of an interim report, always vulnerable to being challenged, corrected, or simply bypassed. The mind searches for a kind of order, but this is a restless, endless process.

(Collini, 2012: 66)

These ten injunctions may represent a counsel of perfection: the University's best self in action. But, I suggest, they also provide an answer to the question of what lies at the heart of 'transformation' claims about the university's effect on its student members. In other words, they represent ways of capturing 'the question of conscience'.

Another important consideration is how far these injunctions are culturally specific. Are they inescapably 'nested' in an inflexible Western, perhaps even an Anglo-Saxon, essentially 'modern' view of the context and of the possibilities of a university culture? Traditional (and complementary) medicine provides one sort of alternative; mysticism (where scientific has to defer to artistic understanding) another; aspects of the Confucian tradition a third (the artist and educator Xu Bing states that 'plagiarism does not exist in Chinese traditional culture'); and the techniques and approaches of postmodernism a fourth. I have discussed above (in Chapter 5) how universities in some traditionally religious societies manage both to reflect and to lead the community's value system, giving the lie to what Habermas calls the problem after the 'French Enlightenment of the eighteenth century' that 'the pluralism of worldviews institutionalized in the liberal state would ultimately marginalize all religious doctrine' (Habermas, 2005: 7). Instead, as he tries to demonstrate, co-existence and co-creation is possible:

For the state, the point is to defuse the social destructiveness of a conflict of worldviews by partially neutralizing their impact on actions and interactions. For the religious community, on the other hand, the fact that the state recognizes the legitimacy of the *persisting* disagreement is important … Through participation in national debates over moral and ethical questions, religious communities can promote a post-secular self-understanding of society as a whole, in which the vigorous continuation of religion in a continually secularizing society must be reckoned with.

(Ibid. 25–6)

That said, most of the commandments will not work where the institution's primary purpose is dogmatic instruction, especially from a doctrinal point of view. At least since the Enlightenment watershed, systematic reference to (and validation by) revealed religion will undermine both the universally agreed mode of inquiry (of knowledge creation, testing, and use) and the intended destination (which for this value system needs always to be provisional). Evolutionary science (and the geological record) is often the acid test. It was acknowledged, for example, by King Abdullah

Bin Abdulaziz Al Saud of Saudia Arabia in opening the new co-educational King Abdullah University of Science and Technology in Thurwal on the Red Sea in 2009, in these words: 'The Islamic Kingdom knows too well that it will not be powerful unless it depends on, after God, science' (quoted in Davis, 2010: 25).

Absent these constraining conditions, the commandments seem to work as a summary of the 'deal' involved in higher education membership in the contemporary world. They include the core role of higher education (what is genuinely 'higher' about it) as a 'conversation' between more and less experienced learners. There is also the vital principle of mutual respect: between staff and student members of the university, between institutions, between national systems, and between universities and their communities.

Chapter 8

Higher education and personal responsibility

My conclusion is approached through a largely philosophical exploration of what it means in the modern world to exercise personal judgement in difficult circumstances. It draws upon the relevant work of contrasting and influential thinkers: Hannah Arendt, Jürgen Habermas, Martha Nussbaum, Elaine Scarry, Samuel Scheffler, Amartya Sen, and Richard Sennett. How important is higher education in our striving for 'public reasoning', for 'thinking what we are doing', and ultimately in 'cultivating humanity'?

Here is the final hard question: is higher education likely to make you better, to improve your capacity to make sound moral as well as technical judgements; in other words to take part in what Sen calls 'public reasoning' (Sen, 2012: 97–8)?

There is clearly a pessimistic, dystopian strain in much contemporary commentary about what higher education does in the world. For a significant group the modern university palpably fails to answer any of the key questions about conscience, character, competence, citizenship, or capability. An example would be the British House of Commons Select Committee inquiry into the 'student experience' of 2009. This exhibited all of the 'autobiographical' dangers of trying to fix the system as it was vaguely remembered from both the members' (and many of their witnesses') perspectives. These included nostalgia and selective memory, a discourse of condescension, and a strong desire to pull up the ladder in defence against the tide of mass higher education (House of Commons, 2009; Watson, 2009: 29–46).

Nor are such voices exclusively from outside the academy. Academics themselves can be curiously unscholarly when considering their own circumstances, especially when looking at others for the source of their discomfort (like 'managers' and politicians) as well as the solution. The adulation with which the community greeted Stefan Collini's 2012 potboiler *What Are Universities For?* is a case in point (Horder, 2012).

Stefan Collini is probably the leading intellectual historian of modern Britain. At its best his work is characterized by breadth of sympathy, meticulous attention to detail, an engaging style, and deep, original insights. These qualities are almost all absent from his commentary on his trade.

I think the problem is the following: Collini writes brilliantly about what he knows, and there are things about which he knows more than anyone else. These include the interior life and times of some our most intriguing intellectual figures over the past two centuries. Another is what it is like to be a scholar in the humanities in one of our ancient universities today, as well as some of those university departments elsewhere which have set their caps at imitating them. That is why the best chapter (quoted twice above) is on the 'character of the humanities' (Collini, 2012: 61–85). Beyond his heartland Collini has been basically reluctant to punt and to guess – until recently. Contrary to a claim in the text (Ibid. 207), over half of this book is recycled from instant commentary on the vicissitudes of government policies and their implementation by the Funding Councils since 1989. It suffers from a lack of disciplined reflection on many of the points made in the heat of the moment.

In *What Are Universities For?* Collini makes mistakes, over-generalizes from idiosyncratic cases, makes complex his own experience while simplifying that of others, and, above all fails to present to his reader not just the diversity but also the richness of contemporary university experience in the round. Some of the errors are significant. The universities created in 1992 don't have charters (Ibid. 31), and being 'higher education corporations' has important implications for their governance and management. The UK system has much more than a 'slight' majority of female participants (the male:female ratio at undergraduate level is now about 40:60, although not at Oxford and Cambridge [Ibid. 32]). Far more influential (as a result of the 1992 Further and Higher Education Act) than the change in status of the polytechnics and Scottish central institutions (the latter don't feature anywhere in Collini's story) was the shift to 'territorial' Funding Councils (Ibid. 34). There has been much more 'reverse academic drift' since the 1980s by traditional universities moving across the ground formerly occupied by the public sector of Higher Education than simple 'academic drift' (or what he calls the 'flow of emulation' [Ibid. 5]) by the latter. Look at where all of the new Business Schools, Faculties of Nursing and Departments of Sports Science have been formed (Ibid. 54). In fact, the Coalition government has not 'accepted the central proposals of the *Browne Review*' (Ibid. 196): Browne recommended uncapping fees, a levy on higher fees, and a return to expansion. The current government has taken the opposite stance on each of these. Perhaps more seriously, Collini has very little to say about science, where the mode of production has managed to defeat some of his straw men, especially through 'unofficial' inter-institutional and international collaboration (see the Royal Society, 2011).

Above all, Collini simply doesn't 'get' some of the main features of the democratization of higher education – internationally – since the Second World War in North America and since the 1980s almost everywhere else. These include: universities returning to their roots of responsiveness to the communities that founded them; the discovery of scholarly excellence in surprising places; unanticipated achievement by non-standard students and lifelong learners (no recognition here of the UK's pioneering Open University); the creation of genuinely international campuses; creative adaptations to the internet; and confirmation that it is possible to do more with less. He claims to be in favour of expansion, from which the university system should 'have nothing to fear' (Ibid. 105). However, everything away from the elite heartland is presumed by him to be a lump: focused on market training, striving to be market-sensitive, and thereby philistine.

What Are Universities For? is an instant book. It is designed to catch a number of waves, including resentment at what successive governments have done to the notoriously (necessarily?) prickly world of academia; commercial interest in a topic of wide public discussion; and a personal desire to take a stand. Paradoxically, many of these features were also true of Newman's *The Idea of The University* as it appeared in consolidated form in 1873, and there are aspects of Collini's position, reputation, and intentions that are oddly similar to his exposition here of the master (Ibid. 39–60). In that case Collini urges, modern readers have failed to spot the irreducible confessional drive, or 'dogmatic intent' (Ibid. 44). In Collini's case, religious faith is substituted by an equally powerful sense of personal entitlement.

In a curious, and certainly unintended way, Collini's deeply conservative complaint gives aid and comfort to his corporate opponents. Michael Barber's widely discussed Institute of Public Policy (IPPR) pamphlet of March 2013 uses Norman Davies's metaphor of the invisible, below-the-surface, build-up towards an avalanche to suggest that most of what we rely on in contemporary higher education is doomed, like Soviet authority across Eastern Europe before 1989 (Barber, *et al.*, 2013: 7). In the process he and his two much younger co-authors (products of American elite universities and a brief experience of working in masters-of-the-universe consultancy firms) go much further than even the author of disruptive innovation himself, Clay Christensen, who sees real value in institutional steadiness amid change (Christensen and Eyring, 2011a). Christensen and his co-author Henry Eyring come to similar conclusions to mine in the Preface (above): 'The people best-qualified to decide which traditions must give way are those of us inside the higher education community' (Christensen and Eyring, 2011b).

To change the metaphor, *An Avalanche is Coming* is a 'kitchen-sink' exercise. It combines a series of moral panics about the global market for graduate talent, the claims by some employers that the talent is not there, inexorable increases in fees for traditional courses, the inevitable fall in the earnings premium associated with first degrees, the 'content revolution' provided by internet-based courses (including MOOCs), and the arrival of the 'for-profits', to declare (again) the death of the traditional university.

The overall effect is as scary as Barber's *Instruction to Deliver*, in which he described his success as leader of Tony Blair's 'delivery unit' in reducing public administration to eight key targets, only two of which were met (Barber 2007: 388–9). These were to have cases in Accident & Emergency Departments formally admitted in under four hours (not an inspiring goal for a modern sophisticated health service, but one that caused enormous disruption in hospital management) and making the trains run on time (with disturbing historical echoes – the train companies met it by increasing journey times, so that the London to Brighton journey now takes longer than it did a century ago). Scanning across the HE scene *Avalanche* expounds a number of half or two-thirds truths, and fails convincingly to combine them into either a coherent vision or a practical call for action. It is also full of the wisdom of the last person Barber spoke to, notably Steve Smith, Vice-Chancellor of a lower-ranked Russell Group university and David Glance of the University of Western Australia's Centre for Software Practice (see website).

There are two calls to arms: 'unbundling' provision and better understanding 'costs and quality'. It is arguable that students and the more responsive institutions are already doing the former, and the solution to the later lies outside the system (especially among employers) – and students understand it all too well (their disdain for online learning is evident [Barber, *et al.*, 2013: 43]). The pamphlet describes one of the co-authors, Saad Rizvi searching for his ideal institutional setting across 'Pakistan, the US, UK, Canada and Singapore'. He chooses Yale (Ibid. 10). The bottom line is that – if the account in this book is at all persuasive – what explains the extraordinary system of the university system, as it developed in Europe and has been imitated elsewhere, is that it does not do avalanches. It does adaptation; it does colonization; it does mergers and acquisitions; it does proximate development. This is broadly how it responded to humanism and the Protestant Reformation in the sixteenth century, to the Industrial Revolution in the early nineteenth century, to the internet in the late twentieth century; and how it is now absorbing developments like for-profit providers, the rise of the 'emerging markets', and even MOOCs.

Back inside the academy, it is instructive to contrast Collini's somewhat bitter dystopia with the tone of the North American counterpart set out in Andrew Delbanco's *College* (discussed in chapters 2, 3, and 7). Delbanco, another literary scholar, is much better at the big historical picture of higher education development. Like Sennett, and other writers drawn on in this chapter, he has a more rounded feel for the potential breadth, and not just the depth, of knowledge. His self-critical gene is more active; he has suggestions beginning at home on how to put things right ('if good things are to happen to students, faculty must care' [Delbanco, 2012: 166)). Above all he has a glimmer of optimism about the future.

I also wish to take the more positive view. For me, in terms of public reasoning and personal responsibility there are two key existential questions going on. Does higher education assist with the process of self-creation, and does it enable its participants better to 'connect' (another 'c' in the spirit of E.M. Forster's *Howard's End*)?

Self-creation links strongly to the notion of personal 'authenticity', which is itself contested. As Neil Levy points out:

> There are conceptions of authenticity that emphasise not self-*discovery* – listening to an inner voice to discover the manner of being that is distinctively one's own – but self-*creation*.
>
> (Levy: 2011, 311)

In other words – in the HE context – a student might not only discover herself, but change in some significant way that person who is discovered. (Levy also points to the objections to this kind of thinking in the work of Jean-Paul Sartre, for whom the acceptance that we might each have an individual essence is the denial of freedom).

Hannah Arendt offers a cautionary riposte about education and the ability to 'connect'. At the heart of her concerns were the dangers of 'superfluousness' in the human condition. This was a concept that she found at its most extreme in the concentration camp, as she described it in her most famous early work, *The Origins of Totalitarianism* (1951):

> Men insofar as they are more than animal reaction and fulfillment of functions are entirely superfluous to totalitarian regimes. Totalitarianism strives not towards despotic rule over men, but toward a system in which men are superfluous. ... As long as all men have not been made equally superfluous – and this has been accomplished only in concentration camps – the ideal of totalitarian domination has not been achieved.
>
> (Arendt, 1951: 457)

Superfluity denies political action, social sense and the essence of humanity. It can be found in ethnic cleansing in the Balkans, in tribal genocide in Africa, and the third generation of statelessness in refugee camps in the Middle East. Eric Hobsbawm famously called the twentieth century 'the age of extremes'. It is hard to see our new century as reducing those extremes.

Arendt's vital personal contribution is about the nature of personal judgement in these circumstances: a drive that I have argued comes close to characterizing all of her philosophical work. In the second volume of her unfinished work, *The Life of the Mind* (1978), on 'thinking' she speculates that:

> If ... the ability to tell right from wrong should turn out to have anything to do with the ability to think, then we should be able to 'demand' its exercise from every sane person, no matter how erudite or ignorant, intelligent or stupid, he may happen to be. ... Conscience ... is the anticipation of the fellow who awaits you if and when you come home.
>
> (quoted in Watson, 1992: 110, 113)

Faced with the political and moral catastrophes of the twentieth century, Arendt sought to secure a platform from which to understand what had happened to us (what she called 'thinking what we are doing'), the detachment that this implies, as well as the qualifications to assign responsibility and to judge. For example, she writes movingly about the philosophical responsibility exercised by non-participants, who often risked death through this exercise of choice:

The non-participants, called irresponsible by the majority, were the only ones who dared to judge by themselves, and they were capable of doing so not because they disposed of a better system of values or because the old standards of right and wrong were still firmly planted in their mind and conscience but, I would suggest, because their conscience did not function in this, as it were automatic, way ... Their criterion, I think, was a different one: they asked themselves to what extent they would be able to live with themselves after having committed certain deeds; and they decided to do nothing not because the world would be changed for the better, but because only on this condition could they go on living with themselves.

(Watson, 1992: 47)

Arendt's biographer, Elisabeth Young-Bruehl, in her *Why Arendt Matters* has bravely attempted to bring the Arendtian project of 'thinking as such' into responses to more recent 'crimes against human plurality', for example by examining the processes of Truth and Reconciliation in post-conflict societies like South Africa and Rwanda, and the post 9/11 American-led 'War on Terror'. She concludes by echoing Arendt's most powerful statement of personal responsibility: 'I must be true to myself. I must not do anything I cannot live with, that I cannot bear to remember' (Young-Bruehl, 2006: 45, 59, 200).

Meanwhile, Richard Sennett extends the notion of connection through his elevation of dialogic over dialectic exchange: the former emphasizes empathy as the desired outcome rather than the condescension of sympathy (Sennett, 2012a: 14, 127, 128, 277). Self-knowledge is vital. He paraphrases Montaigne: 'if we can be easy with ourselves, we can be easy with others' (Ibid. 277).

For both Arendt and Sennett trained or inculcated 'habit' is critical. How do we prepare ourselves to act morally and with responsibility in difficult situations? This is the central question of Elaine Scarry's *Thinking in an Emergency*. In a closely argued sequence she moves from the 'seduction to stop thinking' to 'the place of habit in acts of thinking'. In fact they are mutually supportive: 'habit is everywhere visible in effective emergency preparation. In turn, thinking ... is profoundly visible in the lineaments of habit' (Scarry, 2011: 81).

Habit in these terms is active and not passive. It implies responsibility as well as respect for established patterns of thought, and I am persuaded by the related argument of Samuel Sheffler's 'infrastructures of responsibility' (Scheffler, 2010).

In his *Equality and Tradition*, Scheffler sets out '[T]he importance of taking seriously those categories of value that seem most firmly entrenched in human life'. His is fundamentally an anti-reductionist approach in which valuing is seen as not simply 'desiring, believing valuable, desiring to desire, or having a particular feeling', but instead 'as comprising a complex syndrome of interrelated dispositions and attitudes, including (at least) certain characteristic types of belief, dispositions to

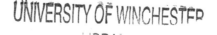

treat certain kinds of considerations and reasons for action, and susceptibility to a wide range of emotions' (Ibid. 4).

These include 'reasons of partiality' which may depend on 'projects', 'relationships' and 'memberships' and this leads to support for 'commonsense' rather than consequentialist morality, as well as the legitimacy of the distinction between doing and allowing (Ibid. 4–5). Another result is 'responsibility-limiting', including being able to prioritize one's own goals over aid to others, and a tension with values like justice, fairness, and equality (Ibid. 5).

The solution is a Rawlsian 'division of moral labour': these big values belong to the 'basic structure' of society, which individuals have a 'duty to support'; but within this framework they may have their 'actions guided by the values appropriate to small-scale inter-personal settings' (Ibid. 6).

In the context of cosmopolitanism, should 'these principles of justice now be applied to the world as a whole rather than to the institutions of individual societies taken one by one'? (Ibid. 6). In response, Scheffler takes 'an intermediate position'. New international institutions 'may require the development of new moral norms'. There follows a critique of 'luck egalitarianism', based on the view that equality is not fundamentally a 'distributive ideal' but a commitment to distributive principles that are appropriate to a society of equals' (Ibid. 7).

He then takes two hard cases. *Terrorism* has 'a distinct moral profile' in that it 'exploits the power of fear in order to undermine the fragile values of social life', while *immigration* establishes that 'under circumstances of large-scale immigration, there is no possibility of preserving unaltered either the imported cultures of immigrant communities or the national cultures of host societies, and that neither side has any general right to such preservation' (Ibid. 8).

This leads to a critique of the notion of 'cultural rights'. '[C]ultures are not perceived sources of normative authority in the same sense that moral, religious, and philosophical doctrines are' (prevalence is not the same as authority). But culture is not the same as 'tradition', which can be authoritative and normative (Ibid. 9), and is 'neither a purely individualistic nor a purely doxastic [relying on personal opinion] phenomenon' (Ibid. 10).

The essays culminate in an analysis of 'The Good of Toleration'. The main problem with toleration is the apparent 'requirement to treat other people's values, which we do not accept, as reasons for modifying our own conduct'. 'A regime of toleration amounts to a practice of mutual deference to one another's values'; however, it can also lead fraternity or solidarity arising from 'the shared experience of subjection to the authority of norms' (Ibid. 10). Empirically, 'intense conflicts of value are ineliminable', but Scheffler concludes optimistically. His optimism is based, first, on acceptance of complexity and rejection of reductionism, and secondly, in the resources of toleration embodied in the liberal tradition (Ibid. 11).

Collectively the chorus of major theoreticians appealed to in this chapter presents an alternative sort of canon for the big question inspiring this book: a modern alternative to St Benedict, Newman, von Humboldt, and the like. From Arendt comes the primacy of thinking leading to both intellectual detachment and social cohesion (avoiding superfluity). Scarry reinforces this through the primacy of habit, and Sennett adds to the authority of the head the engagement of the hand. All three are about coming to terms with modern society, being 'easy' (as in Montaigne), but also understanding the 'big' values (as in Sen and Scheffler) that will lead to toleration. Theodore Zeldin again: 'Nothing is more difficult than to acquire self-confidence without arrogance. It is the basis of all worthwhile achievement' (Zeldin, 1998: 28). Conscience, character, competence, and capability thus converge into a type of cosmopolitan citizenship.

What, in the end, has this book tried to establish about what you do at university, as a student, regardless of your subject and mode of study, or the type of institution, or institutions within which you work? As you study at this level you try to answer some hard questions, some hypothetical, some not. You learn how to work with other people, dead and alive, directly or indirectly (through their work), present or remote. You meet deadlines. You ask yourself why you are doing this, and what difference doing it well will make, for yourself and for others. You get a certificate (as a whole, or in stages). You take out a membership.

So my claim is that higher education's purposes come together in terms of self-creation and the authentic life, the habit of thinking deeply, and the capacity to connect with others empathically. In this analysis I have focused deliberately more on the individual outcome than on the contextual or institutional prerequisite, although I am sympathetic to the literature that suggests that institutions can collectively be moral actors (that is part of the argument of Watson 2009; see also Williams, 2006, and Wettersten, 2006).

Despite its long historical and wide geographical sweep, the claims I am trying to make in this book are necessarily provisional and deliberately modest. As hinted throughout, there are too many books about contemporary higher education that are either polemically dystopian ('the world we have lost') or naively utopian ('HE will solve all of our problems'). My aim, in contrast, has been to affirm both a history and a philosophy for the enterprise that is basically open and malleable. It is true that I have identified sticking points – without which 'higher' education does not deserve the assignation, nor 'university' the title. But within this deliberately generous framework quite a lot goes, for students, teachers, institutional leaders, and sponsors. I began by reflecting on 'our trade'. In conclusion, and in the light of both the determining stratigraphy of the higher education story, and the opportunities that each phase of its reinvention have thrown up, I suggest that any of us with influence (moral and otherwise) should follow the adage of Walter Kaufmann's 'humbition' (the combination of humility and ambition), which he allies with the virtues of love, courage, and honesty (Wettersten, 2006: 282).

To come to a final question (in Nussbaum's terms): does higher education 'cultivate humanity'? (Nussbaum, 1997). Like Delbanco and Scheffler, I can respond optimistically. The simple answer has to be that it can; that it doesn't necessarily do so; and that there are other honourable ways of achieving the same end. It has, however, as I have tried to show in this book, over a number of centuries, and by worrying away at a key set of questions (for which 'conscience' is as good a metaphor as any) been generally good at this important job. At the end of the day everyone makes sense of his or her own higher education, not necessarily immediately, and in some cases not for a considerable time. You don't have to buy the full proposition if you don't want to: there is a definite 'escape clause' (away from doctrinal study) that says that no one can make you take away what you don't want to. You are, however, compelled by an authentic higher education experience to practise answering difficult questions; you are given a safe place in which to do so; depending on your subject or discipline (or combination of these) you will gain a powerful evaluative toolkit; and you will be required to communicate what you have learned. This is hard work, but for centuries participants have found it to be immensely satisfying and it has, generally, helped to make the world a better place.

References

Abramovych, O. (2012) 'Corruption schemes in Ukrainian education system'. *Kyiv Post*, 11 May.

Adams, J., and Smith, D. (2007) 'Higher education, research and the knowledge economy: From Robbins to the Gathering Storm'. In Watson, D., and Amoah, M. (eds) (2007), 81–108.

Agarwal, A. (2013) 'Online universities – time for teachers to join the revolution'. *The Observer*, 16 June.

Alberge, D. (2013) 'Isaiah Berlin despaired of "growth of barbarism"'. *The Observer*, 16 June.

Allen, R., and Layer, G. (1995) *Credit-based Systems as Vehicles for Change in Universities*. London: Kogan Page.

Alter, R. (2010) *Pen of Iron: American prose and the King James Bible*. Princeton, NJ, and Oxford: Princeton University Press.

American Academy of Arts and Sciences (AAAS) (2013) *The Heart of the Matter: The humanities and social sciences for a vibrant, competitive and secure nation*. Cambridge, MA: AAAS.

Appiah, K. (2006) *Cosmopolitanism: Ethics in a world of strangers*. London: Allen Lane.

Arendt, H. (1951) *The Origins of Totalitarianism*. London: Andre Deutsch.

— (1978) *The Life of the Mind*. Ed. McCarthy, M. London: Secker and Warburg.

Arthur, J., with Bohlin, K. (eds) (2005) *Citizenship and Higher Education: The role of universities in communities and society*. London and New York: RoutledgeFalmer.

Arvanitakis J., and Hodge, B. (2012) 'Forms of engagement and the heterogeneous citizen: Towards a reflexive model for youth workshops'. *Gateways: International Journal of Community Research and Engagement*, 5, 56–75.

Ashby, E. (1969) 'A Hippocratic oath for the academic profession'. *Minerva*, 8 (1), 64–6.

Ashby, E., and Anderson, M. (1970) *The Rise of the Student Estate in Britain*. London and Basingstoke: Macmillan.

Ashwin, P., Abbas, A., and McLean, M. (2011) 'A bad deal for "consumers"'. *Times Higher Education*, 17 November.

Asian University for Women (AUW) (2012) 'About the Asian University for Women'. *AUW News*, 5 (1) (October), 2.

Atwood, M. (2008) *Payback: Debt and the shadow side of wealth*. London: Bloomsbury.

Azevedo, A. (2012) 10 Highly Selective Colleges Form Consortium to Offer Online Courses. *Chronicle of Higher Education*, 15 November.

Baggini, J. (2008) *Complaint: From minor moans to principled protest*. London: Profile.

Baldwin, S. (2010) *Robert Recorde: A short account of his life and works*. Tenby: Museum and Art Gallery.

Bamber, V., Trowler, P., Saunders, M., and Knight, P. (2009) *Enhancing Learning, Teaching, Assessment and Curriculum in Higher Education*. Maidenhead: SRHE and Open University Press.

Barber, M. (2007) *Instruction to Deliver: Tony Blair, the public services and the challenge of achieving targets*. London: Politico's.

Barber, M., Donnelly, K., and Rizvi, S. (2013) *An Avalanche is Coming: Higher education and the revolution ahead*. London: IPPR.

Barkham, P. (2010) 'Cambridge and me: how the world's best university changed my life', *The Guardian*, 9 September.

Barnett, R. (1994) *The Limits of Competence: Higher education, knowledge and society*. Maidenhead: SRHE and Open University Press.

— (2007) *A Will to Learn: Being a student in an age of uncertainty*. Maidenhead: SRHE and Open University Press.

— (2011) *Being a University*. London: Routledge.

— (2013) *Imagining the University*. London: Routledge.

Bartlett, T. (2012) 'Harvard sociologist says his research was twisted'. *Chronicle of Higher Education*, 15 August.

Basbøll, T., and Fuller, S. (2008) 'Epistemic convenience: An interview with Steve Fuller'. *Ephemera*, 8 (3), 294–302.

Beard, M. (2009) *It's a Don's Life*. London: Profile Books.

— (2012) *All in a Don's Day*. London: Profile Books.

Beddington, J., Cooper, C., Field, J., Goswami, U., Huppert, F., Jenkins, R., Jones, H., Kirkwood, T., Sahakian, B., and Thomas, S. (2008) 'The mental wealth of nations'. *Nature*, 455 (23 October), 1057–60.

Behrens, R. (2010) 'Interview', Association of University Administrators *Newslink*, 66 (Summer), 7.

Benson, L., Harkavy, I., and Puckett, J. (2007) *Dewey's Dream: Universities and democracies in an age of education reform*. Philadelphia: Temple University Press.

Bergman. J. (2012) 'A U.S. degree at any cost'. *Time*, 27 August, 58–9.

Bidwell, A. (2013) 'Under California bill, faculty-free college would award exam-based degrees'. *Chronicle of Higher Education*, 2 April.

Birnbaum, R. (2004) *Speaking of Higher Education*. Westport, CT, and London: Praeger.

Blair, T. (2008) 'An alliance of values'. *International Herald Tribune*, 19 December, 8.

Blanden, J., Gregg, P., and Machin, S. (2005) *Intergenerational Mobility in Europe and North America: A report supported by the Sutton Trust*. London: Centre for Economic Performance.

Blum, L. (2007) Letter to the Editors. *New York Review of Books*, 26 April, 66.

Booth, R. (2013) 'From Kipling to Python via Thatcher: the pub quiz to get you a passport'. *The Guardian*, 28 January, 3.

Bradbury, M. (1975) *The History Man*. London: Picador.

Bradsher, K. (2013) 'Assembly line? No, thanks'. *International Herald Tribune*, 26–7 January, 2.

Bridges, P., and Flynn, M. (2010) *Making Sense of Credit and Qualification Systems in the UK*. Derby: UK Credit Forum.

British Academy (2004) *'That Full Complement of Riches': The contributions of the arts, humanities and social sciences to the nation's wealth*. London: British Academy.

— (2008) *Punching Our Weight: The humanities and social sciences in public policy-making*. London: British Academy.

— (2010) *Past, Present and Future: The public value of the humanities and social sciences*. London: British Academy.

Brooks, P. (2011) 'Our universities: How bad? How good?' *New York Review of Books*, 24 March, 10–13.

Broughton, P. (2008) *What They Teach You at the Harvard Business School: My two years inside the cauldron of capitalism*. London: Viking.

Broughton, Z. (2006) 'Cagey questions'. *The Guardian*, 22 November.

Brown, G. (2004) 'Britishness'. Speech at the British Council, London, 7 July.

Brown, P., Lauder, H., and Ashton, D. (2011) *The Global Auction: The broken promises of education, jobs and income*. New York: Oxford University Press.

Cadwalladr, C. (2012) 'Goodbye to all this?' *The Observer*, 11 November, Review.

Cahn, S. (ed.) (2011) *Moral Problems in Higher Education*. Philadelphia: Temple University Press.

Carnegie Foundation for the Advancement of Teaching (1990) *Campus Life: In search of community*. Princeton, NJ: Carnegie Foundation.

Carter, I. (1990) *Ancient Cultures of Conceit: British university fiction in the post-war years*. London: Routledge.

Cassels, J. (1990) *Britain's Real Skill Shortage, and What to Do about It*. London: Policy Studies Institute.

Chadwick, O. (1983) *Newman*. Oxford: Oxford University Press.

Christensen, C., and Eyring, H. (2011a) *The Innovative University: Changing the DNA of higher education from the inside out*. San Francisco: Jossey-Bass.

— (2011b) 'How to save the traditional university, from the inside out'. *Chronicle of Higher Education*, 24 July.

Clark, B. (1970) *The Distinctive College*. Chicago: Aldine Press.

— (1998) *Creating Entrepreneurial Universities: Organizational patterns of transformation*. Oxford: Pergamon.

Cloughton, A. (2011) 'Liverpool's free university harnesses anger at the government'. *The Guardian*, 31 August.

Colley, L. (2012) 'North and South'. *London Review of Books*, 2 August, 8.

Collini, S. (2012) *What Are Universities For?* London: Penguin.

Conserving Lakeland (2012) '"Adventure Capital" in the Lake District'. Winter/Spring, 17.

Cook, W. (2010) *Kiss Me Chudleigh: The world according to Auberon Waugh*. London: Hodder and Stoughton.

Côté, J. (2002) 'The role of identity capital in the transition to adulthood: The individualization thesis examined'. *Journal of Youth Studies*, 5 (2) (June), 117–34.

Council for Industry and Higher Education (CIHE) (2008) *Global Horizons and the Role of Employers*. London: CIHE.

Cowen, L. (2011) 'Antioch to give degrees when it reopens in the fall'. *Huffington Post*, 6 May.

Cunningham, B. (ed.) (2008) *Exploring Professionalism*. London: Institute of Education.

Daniel, J. (1996) *The Mega-Universities and Knowledge Media*. London: Routledge.

Davis, G. (2010) *The Republic of Learning: Higher education transforming Australia*. Sydney: HarperCollins.

Dearing, R. (1996) *A Review of Qualifications for 16–19 Year Olds: Full report*. London: School Curriculum and Assessment Authority (SCAA).

De La Baume, M. (2013) 'Paris's plan for more English rings alarm bells'. *International Herald Tribune*, 25–6 May, 3.

Delbanco, A. (2007) 'Scandals of higher education'. *New York Review of Books*, 29 March, 42–7.

— (2012) *College: What it is, was and should be*. Princeton, NJ, and Oxford: Princeton University Press.

Department for Education and Employment (DfEE) (1998) *The Learning Age: A renaissance for a new Britain*. London: HMSO.

DeSantis, N. (2013a) 'Most students in Harvard teaching scandal were forced to withdraw'. *Chronicle of Higher Education*, 1 February.

— (2013b) 'German education minister is stripped of doctorate after plagiarism inquiry'. *Chronicle of Higher Education*, 5 February.

De Wit, H., Ferenez, I., and Rumbley, L. (2103) 'International student mobility: European and US perspectives'. *Perspectives: Policy and practice in higher education*, 17 (1), 17–23.

Di Paolo, T., and Pegg, A. (2012) 'Credit transfer amongst students in contrasting disciplines: Examining assumptions about wastage, mobility and lifelong learning'. *Journal of Further and Higher Education*, 36, 1–17.

Economist, The (2011) 'Testing times'. 31 December.

— (2012a) 'Capital values'. 21 July.

— (2012b) 'A campus tale in Paris'. 1 December.

Education Reform Act (1988). Online. www.legislation.gov.uk

Elon, A. (2002) *The Pity of It All: A portrait of Jews in Germany, 1743–1933*. London: Allen Lane.

Facer, K. (2011) *Learning Futures: Education, technology and social change*. London: Routledge.

Farrar, L. (2013) 'China bans 7 topics in university classrooms'. *Chronicle of Higher Education*, 20 May.

Fazackerley, A. (2013) 'What to do next if you're too cool for university?' *The Guardian*, 18 March.

Feinstein, L., Budge, D., Vorhaus, J., and Duckworth, K. (2008) *The social and personal benefits of learning: A summary of key research findings*. London: Centre for Research on the Wider Benefits of Learning, Institute of Education.

Fernández-Armesto, F. (2011) 'Life and death lessons', *Times Higher Education*, 4 August, 19.

Feynman, R. (2005) *Don't You Have Time To Think?* London: Allen Lane.

Fischer, K. (2012) 'Bucking cultural norms, Asia tries liberal arts'. *Chronicle of Higher Education*, 10 February.

Fischman, J. (2012) 'Medical academics could be legally liable for ghostwritten articles'. *Chronicle of Higher Education*, 24 January.

Florida, R. (2002) *The Rise of the Creative Class: And how it's transforming work, leisure, community and everyday life*. New York: Basic Books.

Fox, J. (2012) 'Top ten myths about mass shootings'. *Chronicle of Higher Education*, 19 December.

Fox, J., and Burstein, H. (2010) *Violence and Security on Campus: From preschool through college*. Santa Barbara, CA: Praeger.

Fraser, R., and Thompson, A. (2012) 'The New Artisan'. *Royal Society of Arts (RSA) Journal* (Summer), 26–7.

Freeh, Sporkin, and Sullivan LLP (2012), *Report of the Special Investigative Counsel Regarding the Actions of the Pennsylvania State University Related to the Child Sex Abuse Committed by Gerald A. Sandusky*, 12 July. Online. www.thefreehreportonpsu.com

Freire, P. (1998) *Pedagogy of Freedom: Ethics, democracy, and civic courage*. Lanham, MD: Rowman and Littlefield.

Friend, T. (2010) 'Protest Studies: The State is broke and Berkeley is in revolt'. *New Yorker*, 4 January.

Fry, T. (ed.) (1982) *The Rule of St. Benedict in English*. Collegeville, MN: Liturgical Press.

Frye, N. (1967) 'The knowledge of good and evil'. In Black, M. (ed.) *The Morality of Scholarship, by Northrop Frye, Stuart Hampshire and Conor Cruise O'Brien*. Ithaca, NY: Cornell University Press.

Furlong, J. (2013) *Education – an anatomy of the discipline: Rescuing the university project?* Abingdon: Routledge.

Futuretrack (2012) *Stage 4: transitions into employment, further study and other outcomes*. Full Report: Warwick Institute for Employment Research (IER) and Higher Education Careers Services Unit (HECSU). Online. www.hecsu.ac.uk

Gardner, H. (ed.) (2007) *Responsibility at Work: How leading professionals act (or don't act) responsibly*. San Francisco: Jossey-Bass.

Gardner, H. (2011) *Truth, Beauty, and Goodness Reframed: Educating for the virtues in the twenty-first century.* New York: Basic Books.

— (2012) 'Harvard's cheating scandal as a play in four acts'. *Cognscenti*, 2 October. Online. http://cognoscenti.wbur.org/

Gardner, L., and Young, J. (2013) 'California's move toward MOOCs sends shock waves but key questions remain unanswered'. *Chronicle of Higher Education*, 14 March.

Garner, H. (2009) 'Publication Integrity Quantified'. *Office of Research Integrity Newsletter*, 17 (4), 1; 6. Online. http://ori.hhs.gov

Garrod, N., and Macfarlane, B. (eds) (2009) *Challenging Boundaries: Managing the integration of post-secondary education.* New York: Routledge.

Garton Ash, T. (2012) 'Freedom and diversity: A liberal pentagram for living together'. *New York Review of Books*, 22 November, 33–6.

Gawande, A. (2007) *Better: A surgeon's notes on performance.* New York: Picador.

Gerstmann, E., and Streb, M (eds) (2006) *Academic Freedom at the Dawn of a New Century: How terrorism, governments, and culture wars impact free speech.* Stanford, CA: Stanford University Press.

Glassner, B., and Schapiro, M. (2013) 'College presidents: Bruised, battered, and loving it'. *Chronicle of Higher Education.* 11 February.

Goldacre, B. (2005) 'Don't dumb me down'. *The Guardian*, 8 September.

Golden, D. (2007) *The Price of Admission: How America's ruling class buys its way into elite colleges and who gets left outside the gates.* New York: Three Rivers Press.

Grove, J. (2012) 'Russell Group students dominate Erasmus scheme'. *Times Higher Education*, 20 May.

Habermas, J. (2005) 'Equal treatment of cultures and the limits of postmodern liberalism'. *The Journal of Political Philosophy*, 13 (1), 1–28.

Hakim, C. (2011) *Honey Money: The power of erotic capital.* London: Allen Lane.

Hallberg, P., and Lund, J. (2005) 'The business of apocalypse: Robert Putnam and diversity'. *Race and Class*, 46 (4), 53–67.

Hamel, G. (2007) *The Future of Management.* Boston: Harvard Business School Press.

Harvie, C. (1976) *The Lights of Liberalism: University liberals and the challenge of democracy.* London: Allen Lane.

Hauser, C., and O'Connor, A. (2007) 'Virginia Tech shooting leaves 33 dead'. *New York Times*, 16 April.

Heller, D., and D'Ambrosio, M. (2008) *Generational Shockwaves and the Implications for Higher Education.* Cheltenham: Edward Elgar.

Henderson, M. (2012) *The Geek Manifesto: Why science matters.* London: Bantam Press.

Hermann, J. (2013) 'University Challenge'. *Evening Standard*, 19 February, 20–1.

Higher Education Academy (HEA) (2011) *The UK Professional Standards Framework for teaching and supporting learning in higher education.* York: HEA.

Higher Education Funding Council for England (HEFCE) (2012) *Research Integrity Concordat: Consultation on proposed implementation from 2013/14.* December. Online. www.hefce.ac.uk

Higher Education Policy Institute (HEPI) (2005) *The Student Experience Report.* London: Unite.

— (2006a) *The Prosperity of English Universities: Income growth and the prospects for new investment.* Oxford: HEPI, 7 September.

— (2006b) *The Academic Experience of Students in English Universities: 2006 Report.* Oxford: HEPI, 31 October.

— (2007) *The Academic Experience of Students in English Universities: 2007 Report.* Oxford: HEPI, 25 September.

— (2009) *The Academic Experience of Students in English Universities: 2009 Report.* Oxford: HEPI Report Summary 40 (May).

— (2012) *The Academic Experience of Students in English Universities: 2012 Report.* Oxford: HEPI Report Summary 57 (May).

— (2013) *The Academic Experience of Students in English Institutions: 2013 Report.* Oxford: HEPI Report Summary 61 (May).

Hobsbawm, E. (2013) *Fractured Times: Culture and society in the twentieth century.* London: Little, Brown.

Hockenos, P. (2013) 'High-profile plagiarism prompts soul-searching in German universities'. *Chronicle of Higher Education,* 25 February.

Holdaway, X. (2012) 'Deceit and fraud: Totally hilarious'. *Chronicle of Higher Education,* 9 August.

Hoover, E. (2013) 'Scholarship providers lead way in measuring character'. *Chronicle of Higher Education,* 20 January.

Horder, T. (2012) 'Who's to blame?' *The Oxford Magazine,* 322, 1–2.

Horowitz, H.L. (1987) *Campus Life: Undergraduate cultures from the end of the eighteenth century to the present.* New York: Knopf.

Hotson, H. (2011) 'Short cuts'. *London Review of Books,* 2 June.

House of Commons: Innovation, Universities, Science and Skills Committee (2009) *Students and Universities.* Eleventh Report of Session 2008–9, 20 July. London: HMSO.

Ibraheem, H. (2013) 'Tightrope act over campus "swamp"'. *Times Higher Education,* 13 June.

IRHEFSF (Independent Review of Higher Education Funding and Student Finance) (2010) *Securing a Sustainable Future for Higher Education*: 14. Online. www.bis.gov.uk/assets/biscore/corporate/docs/s/10-1208-securing-sustainable-higher-education-browne-report.pdf

Institute for Public Policy Research (IPPR) (2013) *A Critical Path: Securing the future of higher education in England.* London: IPPR.

Jacobs, A. (2010) 'Rampant fraud and dishonesty imperil China's brisk ascent'. *New York Times,* 17 October.

Jennings, R. (2010) 'China's "ant tribe" poses policy challenge for Beijing'. *Reuters,* 18 February. Online. www.reuters.com

Jump, P. (2012) 'Something rotten in the state of Spain say whistleblowers'. *Times Higher Education,* 9 August.

Kamenetz, A. (2010) *DIY U: Edupunks, edupreneurs, and the coming transformation of higher education.* White River Junction, VT: Chelsea Green.

Karabel, J. (2005) *The Chosen: The hidden history of admission and exclusion at Harvard, Yale, and Princeton.* New York: Houghton Mifflin.

Kassam-Remtulla, A. (2012) 'Muslim Chaplaincy on Campus: Case studies of two American universities'. DPhil thesis, University of Oxford.

Kellaway, L. (2009) 'School exams fail the office test'. *Financial Times,* 14 June.

Kennedy, D. (1997) *Academic Duty.* Cambridge, MA: Harvard University Press.

Kenyon Jones, C. (2008) *The People's University: 150 years of the University of London and its external students.* London: University of London External System.

Kiss, E., and Euben, J. P. (eds) (2010) *Debating Moral Education: Rethinking the role of the modern university.* Durham, NC, and London: Duke University Press.

Kolowich, S. (2013) 'Harvard professors call for greater oversight of MOOCs'. *Chronicle of Higher Education,* 24 May.

Kors, A., and Silverglate, H. (1998) *The Shadow University: The betrayal of liberty on America's campuses.* New York: Free Press.

Kuhn, T. (1962) *The Structure of Scientific Revolutions*. Chicago: University of Chicago Press.

Lang, J. (2012) 'The grounded curriculum: how can our courses and our teaching capitalize on the benefits of a physical campus?' *Chronicle of Higher Education*, 3 July.

Lay, S. (2004) *The Interpretation of the Magna Charta Universitatum and its Principles*. Bologna: Bononia University Press.

Leibowitz, B. (ed.) (2013) *Higher Education for the Public Good: Views from the South*. London: IOE Press.

Leitch, S. (2006) *Prosperity for All in the Global Economy: World class skills*. London: The Stationery Office.

Leith, S. (2011) *You talkin' to me? Rhetoric from Aristotle to Obama*. London: Profile.

Levi, A. (1971) Introduction to *Praise of Folly and Letter to Martin Dorp (1515) by Erasmus of Rotterdam*. Harmondsworth: Penguin.

Levy, N. (2011) 'Enhancing authenticity'. *Journal of Applied Philosophy*, 28 (3), 308–18.

Lewis, H. (2007) *Excellence without a Soul: Does liberal higher education have a future?* New York: Public Affairs.

Lindsey, U. (2012) 'NYU-Abu Dhabi behaves like careful guest in foreign land'. *Chronicle of Higher Education*, 3 June.

Liu, J. (2012) 'Hong Kong debates "national education" classes'. *BBC News*, 1 September. Online. www.bbc.co.uk

London Economics (2013) *What's the Value of a UK Degree?* Report for Million+ *Behind the Headlines* series. Online. www.millionplus.ac.uk

Lucas, B., Spencer, E., and Claxton, G. (2012) *How to Teach Vocational Education: A theory of vocational pedagogy*. London: City & Guilds Centre for Skills Development. Online. www.skillsdevelopment.org

Macfarlane, B. (2004) *Teaching with Integrity: The ethics of higher education practice*. London and New York: RoutledgeFalmer.

— (2007) *The Academic Citizen: The virtue of service in academic life*. London: Routledge.

— (2009) *Researching with Integrity: The ethics of academic inquiry*. London and New York: Routledge.

— (2012) 'Re-framing student academic freedom: A capability perspective'. *Higher Education*, 63, 719–32.

Madden, P. (2012) 'What is a tutorial?' *The Oxford Magazine*, 325, 5–6.

Mann, S. (2001) 'Alternative perspectives on the student experience: Alienation and engagement'. *Studies in Higher Education*, 26 (1), 7–19.

Marginson, S. (2010) 'A Confucian Tide'. *The Age*, 23 November.

Mark, M. (2012) 'Gunmen open fire on students at Nigerian university'. *The Guardian*, 2 October.

Marr, A. (2004) *My Trade: A short history of British journalism*. London: Macmillan.

— (2007) *A History of Modern Britain*. London: Macmillan.

Matt, S., and Fernandez, L. (2013) 'Before MOOCs: "Colleges of the Air"'. *Chronicle of Higher Education*, 23 April.

Matthews, D. (2012) 'Boom and Bust'. *Times Higher Education*, 5 January.

Mavrogordatos, G. (2012) 'Styx and Stones'. *Times Higher Education*. 24 May.

McIlrath, L., and Mac Labhrainn, I. (eds) (2007) *Higher Education and Civic Engagement: International perspectives*. Aldershot: Ashgate.

McVitty, D., and Morris, K. (2012) *Never Too Late to Learn: Mature students in higher education*. London: Million+ and National Union of Students (NUS). Online. www.millionplus.ac.uk

Mechan-Schmidt, F. (2013) 'Unbridled success: Germany's fee foes claim victory'. *Times Higher Education*, 23 May, 20–1.

Menand, L. (2010) *The Marketplace of Ideas: Reform and resistance in the American University*. New York: W.W. Norton.

— (2011) 'Live and learn: Why we have college'. *The New Yorker*. 6 June, 74–9.

Mény, Y. (2008) *Higher Education in Europe: National systems, European programmes, global issues. Can they be reconciled?* Higher Education Policy Institute (HEPI) Annual Lecture. Online. www.hepi.ac.uk

Miller, S. (2006) *Conversation: A history of a declining art*. New Haven, CT, and London: Yale University Press.

Milmo, C. (2012) 'Young historians "are damaging academia" in their bid for stardom'. *The Independent*. 9 May.

Mintzberg, H. (2009) *Managing*. Harlow: Pearson Education.

Mitchell, D. (2010) 'Three Years dossing at university? It's the only way to train for life', *The Observer*, 22 August.

Morgan, J. (2009) 'Bologna not to the taste of Austrians and Germans'. *Times Higher Education*, 31 December.

— (2012a) 'College of Law sale sets legal precedent for raising of funds'. *Times Higher Education*, 26 April.

— (2012b) 'College of Law becomes UK's first for-profit university'. *Times Higher Education*, 22 November.

— (2012c) 'Reprieve for students as judge says London Met can seek judicial review'. *Times Higher Education*, 21 September.

Morita, L. (2012) 'English and intercultural interaction in the internationalisation of a Japanese university'. *Journal of Intercultural Communication*. Online. www.immi.se/intercultural

Muborakshoeva, M. (2013) *Islam and Higher Education: Concepts, challenges and opportunities*. Abingdon and New York: Routledge.

National Committee of Inquiry into Higher Education (NCIHE) (1997) *Higher Education in the Learning Society (The Dearing Report)*. London: HMSO.

National Student Clearinghouse Research Center (NSCH) (2012) *Transfer & Mobility: A national view of pre-degree student movement in post-secondary institutions*. Online. http://pas.indiana.edu

Newman, J.H. (1902) *University Sketches*. With an introduction by George Sampson. First published in 1856 as *The Office and Work of Universities*. London and Newcastle-upon-Tyne: Walter Scott.

Nixon, J. (2008) *Towards the Virtuous University: The moral bases of academic practice*. London and New York: Routledge.

Noble, D. (2002) 'Technology and the commodification of higher education'. *Monthly Review*, 53 (10), 1 March.

Nowikowski, F. (2011) 'Gifted flee to foreign fields as Italy is strangled by blood ties'. *Times Higher Education*, 8 December.

The Nuffield Foundation (2008) *Science Education in Europe: Critical reflections*. London: Nuffield Foundation. Online. www.nuffieldfoundation.org

Nussbaum, M. (1997) *Cultivating Humanity: A classical defense of reform in liberal education*. Cambridge, MA: Harvard University Press.

— (2010) *Not for Profit: Why democracy needs the humanities*. Princeton, NJ, and Oxford: Princeton University Press.

Oakeshott, M. (1989) *The Voice of Liberal Learning*. New Haven, CT: Yale University Press.

O'Day, R. (2009) 'Universities and professions in the early modern period'. In Cunningham, P., Oosthuizen, S., and Taylor, R. (eds) *Beyond the Lecture Hall: Universities and community engagement from the middle ages to the present day*. Cambridge: Faculty of Education and Institute of Continuing Education, 79–102.

O'Keefe, B. (2007) 'UNSW Singapore campus doomed to failure'. *The Australian*, 27 June.

O'Malley, B. (2013) 'Death toll in Aleppo University bombing set to rise'. *University World News*, 16 January.

Open University (2012) 'UK universities embrace the free, open, online future of higher education powered by the Open University'. Press release, 14 December. Online. www.open.ac.uk/business-school/news/archive/futurelearn-launch

Orkodashvili, M. (2010) 'Corruption in higher education: causes, consequences, reforms – the case of Georgia'. *Munich Personal RePEc Archive*, paper 27679, posted 25 December. Online. http://mpra.ub.uni-muenchen.de/27679/

Palfreyman, D. (ed.) (2008) *The Oxford Tutorial: 'Thanks, you taught me how to think'*. Oxford: Oxford Centre for Higher Education Policy Studies (OXCHEPS).

Parr, C. (2013) 'Futurelearn reveals big plans to deliver Moocs on the move'. *Times Higher Education*, 23 May, 9.

Patton, S. (2012) 'My adviser stole my research'. *Chronicle of Higher Education*, 11 November.

Phillips, D. (2012) 'Aspects of education for democratic citizenship in post-war Germany'. *Oxford Review of Education*, 38 (5), 567–81.

Pratt, J. (1997) *The Polytechnic Experiment, 1965–1992*. Buckingham: SRHE and Open University Press.

Pring, R. (2008) 'Fides Quarens Intellectum: Scholastic beginnings'. In Waks, L. (ed.) *Leaders in Philosophy of Education: Intellectual self-portraits*. Rotterdam: Sense Publishers, 185–200.

Ramsden, P., Batchelor, D., Peacock, A., Temple, P., and Watson, D. (2010), *Enhancing and Developing the National Student Survey: Report to HEFCE by the Centre for Higher Education Studies at the Institute of Education*. London: Institute of Education. Online. www.hefce.ac.uk

Ramzy, A. (2012) 'A new school of thought in China'. *Time*, 1 October, 44–6.

Rawnsley, A. (2010) *The End of the Party: The rise and fall of New Labour*. London: Viking.

Robertson, D. (1994) *Choosing to Change: Extending choice and mobility in higher education*. London: Higher Education Quality Council (HEQC).

Rodin, J. (2007) *The University and Urban Revival: Out of the ivory tower and into the streets*. Philadelphia: University of Pennsylvania Press.

Roth, P. (2000) *The Human Stain*. London: Jonathan Cape.

Rothblatt, S. (2012) 'Notes and Footnotes on California as place and metaphor'. *The Oxford Magazine*, 328, 7–9.

Rowland, S. (2008) 'Collegiality and intellectual love'. *British Journal of Sociology of Education*, 29 (3), 353–60.

Royal Society (RS) (2011) *Knowledge, Networks and Nations: Global scientific collaboration in the 21st century*. Policy Document 03/11. London: The Royal Society. Online. http://royalsociety.org

Ryle, G. (1949) *The Concept of Mind*. London: Hutchinson's University Library.

Sabri, D. (2010) 'Absence of the academic from higher education policy'. *Journal of Higher Education Policy*, 25 (2), 191–205.

Salmi, J., and Altbach, P. (2011) 'New "World-Class" Universities: Cutting through the hype'. *Chronicle of Higher Education*, 20 October.

Sander, L. (2013) 'Freshman survey: This year, even more focused on jobs'. *Chronicle of Higher Education*, 24 January.

Scarry, E. (2011) *Thinking in an Emergency*. New York and London: Norton.

Scheffler, S. (2010) *Equality and Tradition: Questions of value in moral and political theory*. New York: Oxford University Press.

Schmidt, P. (2013) 'AAUP sees MOOCs as spawning new threats to professors' intellectual property'. *Chronicle of Higher Education*, 12 June.

Schuller, T. (1998) 'Social Capital and Community-Building'. In Hurley, K., (ed.) *University Continuing Education in Partnership for Development: Proceedings*. UACE Annual Conference 1997. Leeds: Universities Association for Continuing Education.

Schuller, T., Preston J., Hammond, C., Basssett-Grundy, A., and Bynner, J. (2004) *The Benefits of Learning: The impact of education on health, family life, and social capital*. London: RoutledgeFalmer.

Schuller, T., and Watson, D. (2009) *Learning Through Life: Inquiry into the future for lifelong learning*. Leicester: National Institute of Adult Continuing Education.

Schwitzgebel, E. (2009) 'Do ethicists steal more books?' *Philosophical Psychology*, 22 (6), 711–25.

Scott, D., Hughes, G., Burke, P., Evans, C., Watson, D., and Walter, C. (2013) *Learning Transitions in Higher Education*. Basingstoke: Palgrave Macmillan.

Scott, P. (2012) 'Modern entrepreneurial universities and the *Magna Charta Universitatum*: Tensions and synergies'. Keynote address for the conference 'Conversation on Academic Freedom: the *Magna Charta Universitatum* then and now, 1988–2012', Bologna. Mimeo.

Scottish Credit and Qualifications Framework (SCQF) (2003) *An Introduction to the Scottish Credit and Qualifications Framework: 2nd edition*. Glasgow: Scottish Qualifications Agency (SQA). Online. www.sqa.org.uk

Selingo, J. (2012) 'The rise of the double major'. *Chronicle of Higher Education*, 11 October.

Sen, A. (2009) *The Idea of Justice*. London: Allen Lane.

— (2012) 'The global reach of human rights'. *Journal of Applied Philosophy*, 29 (2), 91–100.

Sennett, R. (2006) *The Culture of the New Capitalism*. New Haven, CT, and London: Yale University Press.

— (2008) *The Craftsman*. London: Allen Lane.

— (2012a) *Together: The rituals, pleasures and politics of co-operation*. New Haven, CT, and London: Yale University Press.

— (2012b) 'This is not their problem'. *The Guardian*, 5 July.

Shattock, M. (2006) *Managing Good Governance in Higher Education*. Maidenhead: Open University Press.

— (2008) *Entrepreneurialism in Universities and the Knowledge Economy: Diversification and organizational change in European higher education*. Maidenhead: SRHE and Open University Press.

Shavit, Y., Arum, R., Gamoran, A., and Menachem, G. (eds) (2007) *Stratification in Higher Education: A comparative study*. Stanford, CA: Stanford University Press.

Shaw-Miller, L. (2001) *Clare Through the Twentieth Century*. Lingfield, Surrey: Third Millennium

Sherwood, H. (2012) 'Ehud Barak formally approves West Bank university of Ariel'. *The Guardian*, 26 December.

Showalter, E. (2013) 'Our age of anxiety', *Chronicle of Higher Education*, 8 April.

Shulman, L. (2005) 'The Signature Pedagogies of the Professions of Law, Medicine, Engineering, and the Clergy: Potential lessons for the education of teachers'. Paper presented at the National Research Council Center for Education, Irvine, CA (6–8 February). Online. http://hub.mspnet.org

Silver, H. (2007) *Tradition and Higher Education*. Winchester: Winchester University Press.

Silver, H., and Silver P. (1997) *Students: changing roles, changing lives*. Buckingham: SRHE and Open University Press.

Sims, J. (2010) 'Mechanics' Institutes in Sussex and Hampshire, 1825–75'. Doctoral thesis, Institute of Education, University of London.

Skidelsky, R. (2003) *John Maynard Keynes 1883–1946: Economist, philosopher, statesman*. London: Macmillan.

Smith, C. (2005) 'Understanding trust and confidence: Two paradigms and their significance for health and social care'. *Journal of Applied Philosophy*, 22 (3), 299–316.

Smith, D. (2011) *Managing the Research University*. New York: Oxford University Press.

Smith, J. (1994) 'Gift authorship: a poisoned chalice?' *British Medical Journal*, 309: 1456.

Smith, L., Mayer, J., and Fritschler, A. (2008) *Closed Minds? Politics and ideology in American universities*. Washington DC: Brookings Institution Press.

Smith, Z. (2012) *NW*. London: Hamish Hamilton.

Snow, C.P. (1959) *The Two Cultures*. Cambridge: Cambridge University Press.

Social and Organisational Mediation of University Learning (SOMUL) (2005) *Working Paper 2*. SOMUL: York (December).

Standing, G. (2012) *The Precariat: The new dangerous class*. London: Bloomsbury Academic.

Stein, J. (2013) 'The new greatest generation: Why millennials will save us all'. *Time*, 20 May, 28–35.

Stratford, M. (2012) 'Senate report paints a damning portrait of for-profit higher education'. *Chronicle of Higher Education*, 30 July.

Stroebe, W., and Hewston, M. (2013) 'Social psychology is primed but not suspect'. *Times Higher Education*, 28 February, 34–9.

Surowiecki, J. (2011) 'Debt by degrees'. *The New Yorker*, 21 November, 50.

Sutton Trust (2008) *Wasted talent? Attrition rates of high-achieving pupils between school and university*. London: Sutton Trust. Online. www.suttontrust.com

Swain, H. (2012) 'Will university campuses soon be "over"?' *The Guardian*, 1 October.

Sweeney, S. (2013) *Going Mobile: Internationalisation, mobility and the European Higher Education Area*. York: Higher Education Academy (HEA).

Tapper, T., and Palfreyman, D. (2011) *Oxford, the Collegiate University: Conflict, consensus and continuity*. Dordrecht: Springer.

Taylor, P. (2007) 'Higher Education and Participatory Development'. *Global University Network for Innovation Newsletter*, 26 June. Online. www.guninetwork.org

Temple, P. (2012) 'Managing higher education and the MBA programme'. *London Review of Education*, 10 (3), 317–19.

Tharoor, I. (2012) 'Illiberal arts: Yale's planned campus in Singapore risks undermining the university's values'. *Time*, 15 October, 59.

Thomas, K. (2012) 'Universities Under Attack', *London Review of Books*, 15 December, 9–10.

Thorp, H., and Goldstein, B. (2010) *Engines of Innovation: The entrepreneurial university in the twenty-first century*. Chapel Hill, NC: University of North Carolina Press.

Times Higher Education (*THE*) (2012) *World University Rankings, 2012/13*. 4 October.

Trachtenberg, S. (2009) *Big Man on Campus: A university president speaks out on higher education*. New York and London: Simon and Schuster.

Trow, M. (1974) 'Problems in the transition from elite to mass higher education'. In OECD Education Committee (eds), *Policies for Higher Education*. Paris: Organisation for Economic Cooperation and Development.

Troy, G. (2011) 'Our moral conversation with students'. *Chronicle of Higher Education*, 17 July.

Tubbs, N. (2012) 'The importance of being useless'. *Times Higher Education*. 11 October, 40–3.

Turner, F.M. (2002) *John Henry Newman: The challenge to evangelical religion*. New Haven, CT, and London: Yale University Press.

Universities UK (UUK) (2012) *The Concordat to Support Research Integrity*. London: UUK (July). Online. www.universitiesuk.ac.uk

University of Aberdeen (1906) *Quatercentenary Celebrations, September, 1906: Handbook to city and university*. Aberdeen: University of Aberdeen.

University of Birmingham (2012) 'Multi-million pound award to support first research centre dedicated to understanding the UK's character and values'. Press release, 16 May.

University of London (2011) 'Statement: New College of the Humanities'. Press release, 6 June. Online. www.londoninternational.ac.uk/media/press-releases

University of Oxford (2011) *Financial Statements of the Colleges: year ended 31 July, 2010.*

Unwin, L., Felstead, A., and Fuller, A. (2008) *Learning at Work: Towards more expansive opportunities*. London: Institute of Education.

Utley, T. (2011) 'I spent three years at Cambridge eating walnut cake, but don't let anyone tell you a degree is a waste of time', *Daily Mail*, 26 August.

Vasager, J., Lewis, P., and Watt, N. (2010) 'Student fees protest: "this is just the beginning"'. *The Guardian*, 10 November.

Vick, K., and Khalil, A. (2013) 'Faith and the campus'. *Time*, 10 June, 26–31.

Walker, M. (2006) *Higher Education Pedagogies*. Maidenhead: SRHE and Open University Press.

Walsh, J. (2012) 'A degree is like an Olympic medal: You want a gold not a report card'. *The Independent*, 5 October.

Watson, D. (1989) *Managing the Modular Course: Perspectives from Oxford Polytechnic*. Buckingham: SRHE and Open University Press.

— (1992) *Arendt*. London: HarperCollins.

— (1994) 'Living with Ambiguity: Some dilemmas of academic leadership'. In Bocock, J., and Watson, D., (eds), *Managing the University Curriculum: Making common cause*. Maidenhead: SRHE and Open University Press.

— (2000) *Managing Strategy*. Buckingham: Open University Press.

— (2006) *Who killed what in the quality wars?* No 1. in series *Quality Matters*, Gloucester: QAA. Online. www.qaa.ac.uk

— (2007) *Managing Civic and Community Engagement*. Maidenhead: Open University Press.

— (2008a) *Who owns the university?* No 3. in series *Quality Matters*, Gloucester: QAA. Online. www.qaa.ac.uk

— (2008b) 'Universities behaving badly?' *Higher Education Review*, 40 (3), 3–14.

— (2008c) 'Universities and Lifelong Learning'. In Peter Jarvis (ed.) *The Routledge International Handbook of Lifelong Learning*. London: Routledge, 102–13.

— (2009) *The Question of Morale: Managing happiness and unhappiness in university life*. Maidenhead: Open University Press.

— (2010) 'Universities' Engagement with Society'. In Peterson, P., Baker, E., McGaw, B. (eds) *International Encyclopedia of Education*. Vol. 4, 398–403. Amsterdam and Oxford: Elsevier.

— (2011) 'A Teaching Journey'. In Brown, T. (ed.) *Ten Years of National Teaching Fellowships: Four stories from education*. Bristol: ESCalate (HEA Education Subject Centre), 21–4.

Watson, D., and Amoah, M. (eds) (2007) *The Dearing Report: Ten years on*. London: Institute of Education.

Watson. D., and Bowden, R. (2005) *The Turtle and the Fruit Fly: New Labour and UK higher education*. Brighton: University of Brighton Education Research Centre.

Watson, D., and Maddison, E. (2005) *Managing Institutional Self-Study*. Maidenhead: Open University Press.

Watson, D., Stroud, S., Hollister, R., and Babcock, E. (2011) *The Engaged University: International perspectives on civic engagement*. New York and London: Routledge.

Watt, N. (2012) 'David Cameron fluffs citizenship test on David Letterman's Late Show'. *The Guardian*, 27 September.

Weko, T. (2004) *New Dogs and Old Tricks: What can the UK teach the US about university education?* Oxford: Higher Education Policy Institute (HEPI).

Wettersten, J. (2006) *How Do Institutions Steer Events? An inquiry into the limits and possibilities of rational thought and action.* Aldershot and Burlington, VT: Ashgate.

Wheeler, C. (2013) 'Philosophical element completes comprehensive overhaul'. *Times Higher Education*, 10 January, 20–1.

Which? (2013) *The Student Academic Experience Survey* Policy Report (May). London: Which?

Whitchurch, C. (2013) *Reconstructing Identities in Higher Education: The rise of third space professionals.* SRHE series. London: Routledge.

Willetts, D. (2011) *The Pinch: How the baby boomers took their children's future – and why they should give it back.* London: Atlantic Books.

— (2012) 'A-level results: A day to celebrate'. *The Guardian*, 15 August.

Williams, G. (2006) '"Infrastructures of Responsibility": the moral tasks of institutions'. *Journal of Applied Philosophy*, 23 (2), 207–21.

Williams, G., and Filippakou, O. (2010) 'Higher Education and UK elite formation in the twentieth century'. *Higher Education*, 59 (1), 1–20.

Willis Commission (2012) *Quality with Compassion: The future of nursing education.* Online. www.williscommission.org.uk

Wilton, P. (2011–12) 'Policy Watch', *Professional Manager*, Winter, 17.

Withington, P. (2012) 'Past v. Present'. *London Review of Books*, 10 May, 19.

Wolf, A. (2002) *Does Education Matter? Myths about education and economic growth.* London: Penguin.

Woodward, B. (2005) *The Secret Man: The story of Watergate's Deep Throat.* London: Simon and Schuster.

Wooldridge, E., and Newcomb, E. (2011) *Distinctiveness and Identity in a Challenging HE Environment: A unique opportunity for cathedrals group institutions.* Chester: The Cathedrals Group.

Woolf, H. (2011) *The Woolf Inquiry: An inquiry into the LSE's links with Libya and lessons to be learned.* London: LSE. Online. www.woolflse.com

Worton, M. (2013) 'Big picture from all angles'. *Times Higher Education*, 21 February.

Yong, W. (2010) 'In Iran, future of university is in flux'. *New York Times*, 15 October.

Young, J. (2012a) 'Coursera hits 1 million students, with Udacity close behind'. *Chronicle of Higher Education*, 10 August.

— (2012b) 'Coursera adds honor-code prompt in response to reports of plagiarism'. *Chronicle of Higher Education*, 24 August.

— (2013a) 'Coursera announces details for selling certificates and verifying identities'. *Chronicle of Higher Education*, 9 January.

— (2013b) 'What professors can learn from "hard core" MOOC students'. *Chronicle of Higher Education*, 20 May.

Young, M. (2001) 'Down with meritocracy'. *The Guardian*, 29 June.

Young-Bruehl, E. (2006) *Why Arendt Matters.* New Haven, CT, and London: Yale University Press.

Yu, V. (2011) 'I was a tiger daughter'. *New York Times*, 28 January.

Zeldin, T. (1994) *An Intimate History of Humanity.* London and New York: HarperCollins.

— (1998) *Conversation.* London: Harvill.

List of websites

Anhanguera: www.anhanguera.com/ir

Ashmolean Museum: www.ashmolean.org/about/historyandfuture

Aung San Suu Kyi – acceptance speech: www.ox.ac.uk/media/news_stories/2012/assk_speech_full.html

Boston College HE Corruption Monitor: www.bc.edu/research/cihe/hecm.html

Carnegie classification: http://classifications.carnegiefoundation.org

Connectivist: www.connectivistmoocs.org/what-is-a-connectivist-mooc

Council for Graduate Schools – Project for Scholarly Integrity: www.scholarlyintegrity.org

Coursera: www.coursera.org

Daily Telegraph – plagiarism league table: www.telegraph.co.uk/education/educationnews/8363345/The-cheating-epidemic-at-Britains-universities.html

Degreed: http://degreed.com

European Social Survey: www.europeansocialsurvey.org

European Standards for degrees in nursing: www.euro.who.int/__data/assets/pdf_file/0005/102200/E92852.pdf

Eurostat – youth unemployment (September 2012): http://epp.eurostat.ec.europa.eu/cache/ITY_PUBLIC/3-31102012-BP/EN/3-31102012-BP-EN.PDF

HEFCE Religious Literacy Workshops: www.hefce.ac.uk/news/newsarchive/2012/name,75507,en.html

Heidegger's Rectoral Address: https://webspace.utexas.edu/hcleaver/www/330T/350kPEEHeideggerSelf-Assertion.pdf

Key Information Sets: www.hefce.ac.uk/media/hefce/content/whatwedo/learningandteaching/informationabouthighereducation/keyinformationsets/kis_sample.pdf

James Cook University – mission: www.jcu.edu.au/about/strategic-intent/index.htm

Life in the UK test: http://lifeintheuktest.ukba.homeoffice.gov.uk

Massachusetts Institute of Technology – Open Courseware: http://ocw.mit.edu/index.htm

MOOC Research: www.moocresearch.com

National Student Survey: www.thestudentsurvey.com

Natural Capital: www.naturalcapitalinitiative.org.uk

Notre Dame University – mission: http://nd.edu/aboutnd/history

Pearson College: www.pearsoncollege.com

Quest University: www.questu.ca/about_quest/index.php

Religious Literacy (HEFCE): www.hefce.ac.uk/whatwedo/lgm/lgmprojects/staffdevelopment/religiousliteracyleadershipproject

Skoll Foundation: www.skollfoundation.org

South East England Credit Consortium: www.seec.org.uk

Stanford University – mission: www.stanford.edu/about

Tent City: http://tentcityuniversity.org

The Art of Taking Personal Responsibility: http://taotpr.com

Udemy: www.udemy.com

UK Office of Research Integrity: www.ukrio.org

UnCollege: www.uncollege.org/team

Universities UK (UK) – Research Integrity Concordat: www.universitiesuk.ac.uk

University of Cambridge – Engineering Department: www.eng.cam.ac.uk/125.shtml

University of Nottingham – Ningbo: www.nottingham.edu.cn/en/about/index.aspx

University of Oxford – Engineering Department: www.eng.ox.ac.uk/about-us/history-of-the-department

University of Oxford – Masters in Public Policy: www.bsg.ox.ac.uk/programmes/course-outline

University of Peshawar: www.upesh.edu.pk

University of the Third Age: www.u3a.org.uk

University of Western Australia – Centre for Software Practice: www.csp.uwa.edu.au

Venerable English College, Rome: www.vecrome.org

Yale University – Sheffield Scientific School: www.yale.edu/secretary/programs/sheffield.html

Zaytuna College: www.zaytunacollege.org

All accessed 12 June 2013.

Index